THINK HISTORY! 2

REVOLUTIONARY TIMES
1500–1750

Ros Adams   Denise Waugh   Steve Waugh

Series editor: Lindsay von Elbing

FOUNDATION

heinemann.co.uk
✓ Free online support
✓ Useful weblinks
✓ 24 hour online ordering

01865 888080

Heinemann

Inspiring generations

Heinemann Educational Publishers
Halley Court, Jordan Hill, Oxford, OX2 8EJ
Part of Harcourt Education

Heinemann is the registered trademark of
Harcourt Education Limited

© Ros Adams, Denise Waugh, Steve Waugh, 2003

First published 2003

07 06 05 04 03
10 9 8 7 6 5 4 3 2 1

British Library Cataloguing in Publication Data is available from the British Library on
request.

ISBN 0 435 31351 7

Produced by IFA Design Ltd
Printed in Spain by Mateu Cromo s.a.
Original illustrations © Harcourt Education Limited, 2003

Photographic acknowledgements
The authors and publisher would like to thank the following for permission to reproduce
photographs:
AKG: 8A, 24B, 95H, 98D, 152A, 172C; Art Archive: 11A; Bridgeman Art Library: 8B, 23A, 24C,
29A, 30C, 42D, 51B, 57A, 72B, 85B, 95F, 96K, 97A, 100J, 106K, 111A, 120A, 149D, 165C, 197A,
214G; BAL/Bristol City Art Gallery: 19G; BAL/Guildhall: 34C; BAL/Hatfield House: 93A; Bristol
Museum and Art Gallery: 212B; Christopher Ridley: 31G; Corbis: 8C, 94C; Fotomas Index:
48E, 67B, 73C, 175A, 130A, 133A; Glasgow Museums: 184B; Historical Archive: 133B; Hulton
Getty: 79D, 117C; Mansell Collection: 31F; Mary Evans Picture Library: 12B, 35F, 51A, 108P,
135H, 137B, 139E, 140G; National Library of Scotland: 187A; National Maritime Museum:
173E; National Portrait Gallery: 40C, 45A, 203A, 204B; National Trust: 94D, 96I; Palace of
Westminster Collection: 49F; Peter Newark: 148B, 153C, 214E; Rex: 137A; Ronald Grant: 26A;
The Royal Collection: 85A, 191A; Scala: 104H; Scala/Galleria d'Arte Moderna, Florence: 36H;
Science Photo Library: 197B; Sidney Sussex College, Cambridge: 63A; Topham
Picturepoint: 180A; Viscount de L'Isle/Penshurst Palace: 99H

Source unknown: 47C, 51C, 67A, 68C, 69D, 70A, 77A, 80F, 83B, 102B, 109R, 134F, 154F, 179D

Cover photograph: © The Art Archive. The painting is 'The Battle of Marston Moor' by
James Ward.

Picture research by Veneta Bullen

Tel: 01865 888058   www.heinemann.co.uk

CONTENTS

INTRODUCTION

A painting of Anne Boleyn.

A seventeenth-century print of a witch.

💡 Which one of these is the odd one out? Why?

At this stage, you might want to make a wild guess. You might even be able to make an 'educated guess' based on your Key Stage Two study of history, or from your own general knowledge.

One possible answer is that Oliver Cromwell is the odd one out – he's a man and the other two are women. However, there are many more possibilities, and there is not just one correct answer!

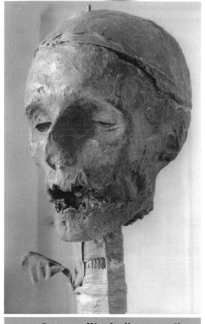

Cromwell's skull on a spike.

The good thing about the game of odd one out is that it makes you *think* about links and connections between things. The more you know about history, the more links and connections you can make. Making links and connections is a very important skill, because the information in this book is organised into three big sections:

1 Religion and internal politics
2 Social life
3 External relations

Quite often, information from one section may overlap with another section, so you will need to think hard! To help you to do this, each big section has its own introduction.

Let's consider the three big sections:

Religion and internal politics

💡 Do you remember finding out about life in the Middle Ages? You probably recall that religion was very important at that time. Can you suggest why?

Between 1500 and 1750 religious beliefs changed a great deal. The picture of Anne Boleyn was chosen to represent religious changes. Turn to pages 6 to 7 and skim read. Can you work out what connects Anne Boleyn with religious changes?

Social life

This theme is to do with how different groups of people in England lived. One of the most interesting events of this period was the witch craze of the seventeenth century.

External relations

Finally, we also need to find out about how England got on with other countries between 1500 and 1750. Cromwell's picture was chosen because he was involved with events between England and Ireland in the seventeenth century.

In the same way that you made links and connections between the three figures in the odd one out activity, you can also make links between the themes. For example, religious changes affected both social life and external relations.

By the end of this book, you should be able to suggest more answers to the odd one out puzzle at the beginning. For a real challenge, you may even want to think about how the information in the book has been organised into three sections. Would you organise the information differently?

THEME: RELIGION AND INTERNAL POLITICS

INTRODUCTION

How many people in your class believe in God? Do many go to church? Probably not many. In the sixteenth and seventeenth centuries almost every English person believed in God and went to church. Religion was very important and it had a big impact on the history of Britain.

Henry VIII wanted a divorce but the Catholic Church would not give him one. So he broke away from the Pope and made himself Head of the Church of England. In the following reigns everything that people were used to changed. People were killed because of what they believed in. Catholics burned Protestants and Protestants killed Catholics. Henry's daughter, Mary, was given the nickname 'Bloody Mary' because she burned many Protestants in her short reign (1553-8). But did she really deserve the name?

Mary, Queen of Scots, was a Catholic but her cousin, Queen Elizabeth I of England, was a Protestant. Mary clamed the throne of England so Elizabeth kept her in prison for almost twenty years. Then she had Mary executed. Did Mary deserve to die?

In the seventeenth century King James I (1603-25), a Protestant, faced opposition from the Catholics. Did Guy Fawkes really try to blow the king up in the Gunpowder Plot - or was he framed? King James I's grandson, James II, was a Catholic. He was very unpopular and after only three years the 'Glorious Revolution' of 1688 forced him off the throne. How 'glorious' was this revolution really?

Religion was even a cause of the Civil War (1642-9), when King Charles I fought parliament for control of England. Who or what was most responsible for this war? When he lost, King Charles I was executed and extreme Protestants called Puritans ran the country. They said that everyone should have their lives ruled by religion.

Religion and arguments about it led to many changes in England in the sixteenth and seventeenth centuries. There were changes in politics, family life, employment, leisure activities, dress, behaviour - in fact there were changes in every part of people's lives. The rich and the poor, men and women, Protestants and Catholics all experienced Revolutionary Times!

TIMELINE 1517-1685

1517	Martin Luther protests against the Catholic Church.	**1603**	James VI of Scotland becomes James I of England.
1527	The Pope does not let Henry VIII get divorced from Catherine of Aragon.	**1605**	Catholics try to blow up James I and Parliament in the Gunpowder Plot.
1534	Henry VIII becomes Head of the Church of England.	**1625**	James I dies and is succeeded by Charles I.
1536	Henry VIII orders all the monasteries in England to be closed.	**1629-40**	Charles I rules without Parliament.
1547-54	Edward VI tries to make England Protestant.	**1642-9**	The English Civil War.
		1649	Trial and execution of Charles I.
1554-58	Mary I tries to make England Catholic.	**1652**	The Puritan Parliament bans the celebration of Christmas.
1558	Elizabeth I becomes queen and tries to find a 'middle way' in religion.	**1658**	Death of Oliver Cromwell.
		1660	Charles II returns from exile. Puritans lose their influence.
1587	Mary, Queen of Scots is beheaded at Fotheringay Castle.	**1685**	Charles II dies and is succeeded by his brother James II.

DID ENGLAND BECOME PROTESTANT IN THE SIXTEENTH CENTURY?

WHY DID HENRY VIII BREAK AWAY FROM THE AUTHORITY OF THE POPE?

Objectives

By the end of this section you will find out:
• why Henry VIII wanted a divorce from Catherine of Aragon
• why this led Henry to break away from the Pope and the Roman Catholic Church.

You will be able to:
• identify examples of cause and effect in the events leading to the break with the Pope and the Roman Catholic Church.

Key words

Heir The next person in line to become king or queen.

Starter

It is 1527. You are Henry VIII and you have a problem.

*You have been married for almost 20 years to Catherine of Aragon. She has not given you a son. She is now too old to have children. You need a male **heir**. You have fallen in love with Anne Boleyn, and you want to marry her.*

What would you do if you were Henry VIII?

SOURCE Ⓐ

Catherine of Aragon.

SOURCE Ⓑ

King Henry VIII of England.

SOURCE Ⓒ

Anne Boleyn.

Possible answers to Henry's problem		
1 Ask the **Pope** for a divorce.	2 Have Catherine killed and marry Anne.	3 Wait until Catherine dies and then marry Anne.

Possible results of these actions		
A Catherine may live longer than you. And if Anne becomes pregnant outside of marriage, your son will be **illegitimate** and so won't be able to become king after you.	**B** The Pope let you marry Catherine in the first place - perhaps he'll let you divorce her. But Catherine's nephew has the Pope in prison. He won't allow the divorce.	**C** Catherine is very popular with the English people - divorcing or killing her would make you very unpopular. Anyway, she hasn't committed a crime.

Which action will produce which result?

What advice do you think Henry got from his ministers?

Why did the problem of Henry's divorce lead to a break with the Pope and the Roman Catholic Church?

Henry's wife, Catherine, had been married to his brother, Arthur. When Arthur died Henry married Catherine. Henry and Catherine had one child - a daughter, Mary. The Bible said it was wrong for a man to marry his brother's widow. Henry thought God was punishing him by not letting him have a son. However, the Pope would not let Henry have a divorce.

Key words

Pope The head of the Catholic Church, who lives in Rome.

Illegitimate A person who is born to parents who are not married.

Archbishop of Canterbury The leading churchman in England.

Henry decided to make himself Head of the Church of England. This meant that Henry did not need the Pope to agree with any decisions he made. The **Archbishop of Canterbury** could now give Henry his divorce. Henry had already secretly married Anne and she was pregnant. Anne became queen. She gave birth ... to a girl.

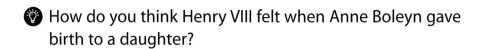 How do you think Henry VIII felt when Anne Boleyn gave birth to a daughter?

Many of the causes of Henry VIII's break with the Pope are closely linked.

1 Work in pairs. In your book, copy the boxes below and draw arrows between two boxes to show how one fact led to another. You must be able to use the words 'and so' to link the two.
Your objective is to get to the box in the middle, while trying to make as many links as you can along the way. **WS**

Henry wanted a male heir.

Henry wanted a divorce from Catherine of Aragon.

Henry believed his marriage to Catherine was sinful.

The Pope wouldn't grant Henry a divorce.

HENRY VIII BROKE WITH THE POPE

Henry made himself Head of the Church in England.

Anne became pregnant.

Henry married Anne.

Catherine could not produce a male heir.

The Pope was a prisoner of Catherine's nephew.

2 When you have finished, compare your decisions with another pair. Who can explain the most links?

Plenary

Here are the answers! Work out the questions.

1 Catherine had previously been married to Henry's brother, Arthur.
2 The Pope.
3 Henry decided to make himself Head of the Church in England.
4 Henry wanted his son to be able to follow him as king.
5 Archbishop Cranmer.

WHAT WAS WRONG WITH THE CATHOLIC CHURCH IN THE SIXTEENTH CENTURY?

By the end of this section you will understand:
- why a growing number of people were unhappy with the Catholic Church in the sixteenth century
- what Protestants thought was wrong with the Catholic Church.

You will be able to:
- explain the main differences between Catholic and Protestant ideas.

Starter

Coins from the reigns of Henry VIII, Edward VI, Mary I and Elizabeth I.

What do these coins have in common?

Look carefully at the words on each coin and you will see that it says F.D. or 'Fid. Def.' - Fidei Defensor. *This is Latin for 'Defender of the Faith'.*

Look at a modern coin and read the words on it. What meaning do you think it has today?

Criticism of the Catholic Church

In 1521 Henry VIII was given the title *Fidei Defensor* by the Pope as a reward for his loyalty in defending the Catholic religion from attack by 'Protestants'. These were people who were protesting against the Catholic Church. Henry put the title on his coins.

But only a few years later, in 1533, Henry argued with the Pope. He made himself Head of the Church of England instead of the Pope.

What was the new protest movement all about?

In 1517 a German monk called Martin Luther made a list of 95 complaints about the Catholic Church. He thought it was wrong that the Church would forgive people's sins in return for money.

Martin Luther.

It was dangerous to criticise the Catholic Church openly. Luther could have been arrested and burned for being a **heretic**. Luther was lucky because the ruler of his country decided to protect him. Luther's ideas spread quickly. Soon his followers (Protestants) began to start churches of their own.

What did it mean to be a Catholic in England at this time?

For people at this time, the church was very important. They believed in God, heaven and hell. They went to church at least once a week. They did not understand the words the priest said because they were in Latin. Church services were full of mystery.

Key words

Heretic A person who follows beliefs which are against the teachings of the Church.

The priest was people's link to God. He told them Bible stories. There were pictures of these on the walls and in the stained-glass windows of the church. People believed that during **Mass** the wine and bread turned into the blood and body of Jesus. Churches also had **relics**, which would help people get closer to God if they touched them.

💡 Why was the priest such an important person to Catholics?

What were the differences between Catholic and Protestant ideas?

Catholics and Protestants are both Christians, but in the sixteenth century they had very different ideas about how to worship. Each side was sure they were right. They were prepared to kill each other for their own religion.

TASKS...

1 a) Look at statements A to H.

A Churches should be beautiful. They should have statues and stained glass windows.

B People need to understand church services and the Bible, so they should be in English.

TASKS...

C People shouldn't be distracted when worshipping God. Churches should be plain and simple.

D There isn't a miracle in Mass. The wine and bread don't change into Jesus's flesh and blood.

E Latin makes the Bible and services special. It has been the language of the Church for hundreds of years.

F A good preacher can help people to understand Bible stories and can explain things to them, but he doesn't need to be set apart - he should get married.

G It is important to obey the Pope. He is God's representative on earth and his priests can help you to get your sins forgiven more quickly when you die.

H During mass a miracle occurs and the wine and bread change into Jesus's flesh and blood.

b) Now look at the drawings showing the insides of a Catholic church and a Protestant church (page 15).

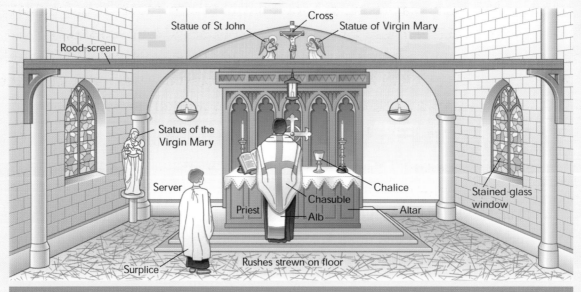

Statue of St John
Cross
Statue of Virgin Mary
Rood screen
Statue of the Virgin Mary
Server
Chalice
Stained glass window
Chasuble
Priest
Altar
Alb
Surplice
Rushes strewn on floor

The inside of a Catholic church.

TASKS...

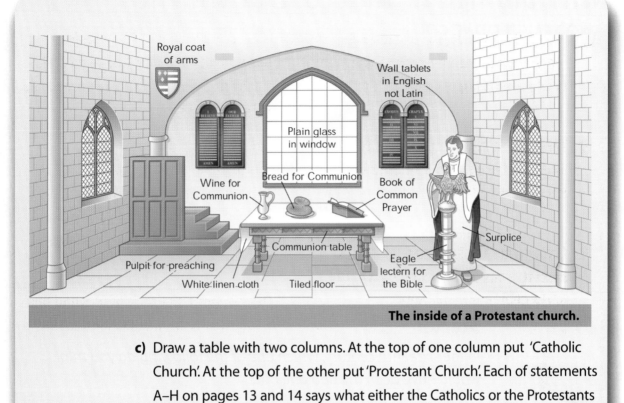

Royal coat of arms

Wall tablets in English not Latin

Plain glass in window

Wine for Communion

Bread for Communion

Book of Common Prayer

Surplice

Communion table

Eagle lectern for the Bible

Pulpit for preaching

White linen cloth

Tiled floor

The inside of a Protestant church.

c) Draw a table with two columns. At the top of one column put 'Catholic Church'. At the top of the other put 'Protestant Church'. Each of statements A–H on pages 13 and 14 says what either the Catholics or the Protestants believed. Sort them out by writing the letters in the correct column. **WS**

Plenary

How many ways can you think of to remember the differences between Catholic and Protestant beliefs? Here is a simple memory jogger to help you: 'Pure Protestants and Complicated Catholics', which shows that the Protestants wanted to make the Church simple, while the Catholics wanted to keep all the ornaments and decorations.

You could also try making up a story using key words, or perhaps even a poem or a song.

WHY DID HENRY VIII CLOSE DOWN THE MONASTERIES?

Objectives

By the end of this section you will know:
- how and why Thomas Cromwell closed down the monasteries in England
- what was wrong with the monasteries
- why many people were worried about the **dissolution** of the monasteries
- how Henry dealt with the Pilgrimage of Grace.

Starter

In the sixteenth century, which one of the following do you think would have been the odd one out:

- *a hotel*
- *a prison*
- *a hospital*
- *a meditation centre*
- *a school?*

Here is a clue! A monastery would have been all but one of these things.

What led to the dissolution of the monasteries?

Henry's divorce was not the only problem he had. He had stopped sending **taxes** to the Pope but he was still spending far too much money. Henry liked eating, drinking and parties. He had also fought a war against France. And after Henry broke with the Pope he was worried that the Catholic countries of Europe might attack England.

Key words

Dissolution Breaking something up.
Taxes Money paid to a ruler or government by the people.

 How could Henry get more money?

A lot of people in England thought the break with the Pope was wrong, which annoyed Henry. Most monks and nuns were loyal to the Pope as leader of the Church, not to the king. Henry wanted everyone to be loyal to him.

Henry also needed money so, in 1536, he told his chief minister, Thomas Cromwell, to start closing down the monasteries. Over the years many monks had begun to ignore their **vows** of **poverty** and **chastity**. Some lived lives of luxury. Many monasteries owned a lot of land. They had gold crosses and cups, beautiful pictures, and expensive Bibles. Even the buildings were valuable - the lead on the roof was worth a lot of money.

However, monasteries also helped a lot of people. They were:

Key words

Vow A promise which says that a person will behave in a certain way.
Poverty Being poor. Monks made a promise to God to be poor. This showed how religious they were.
Chastity Being pure of body, which includes not having sexual intercourse.

• Hotels. They gave travellers food and shelter.

• Schools. They taught boys how to read and write.

• Hospitals. They looked after the sick.

If monasteries were so useful, why did Henry close them down?

Thomas Cromwell needed a good excuse to close the monasteries down. He did not want to make the king unpopular. So he sent inspectors round the country to report on what was wrong with the monasteries. He asked them to say how well-behaved the monks and nuns were and how rich the monasteries were. Cromwell chose inspectors who were not loyal Catholics.

Before you read the inspectors' reports, what do you think the inspectors found out about the monasteries?

Do you think the inspectors' reports on the monasteries would be fair?

What can we tell about the state of the monasteries from historical evidence?

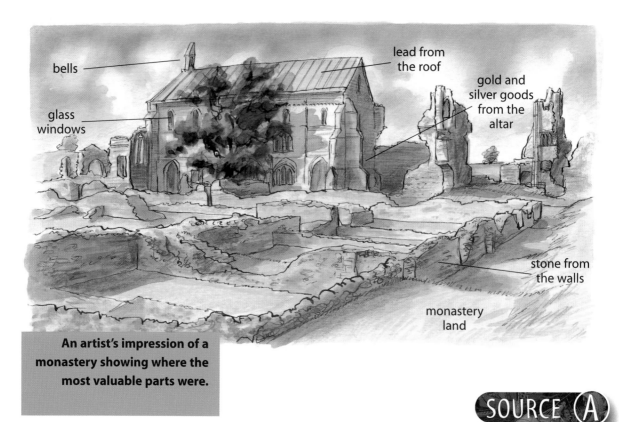

bells

glass windows

lead from the roof

gold and silver goods from the altar

stone from the walls

monastery land

An artist's impression of a monastery showing where the most valuable parts were.

Key words

Habit A monk's robe.
Celibate Living as a single person and not having sexual relations.

Monks and nuns were supposed to live like Jesus's followers.
They should:

* give everything they had away and be poor
* wear a **habit** and eat simple food
* stay **celibate**
* look after the poor, the sick and travellers
* behave in a Christian way
* worship and pray several times a day
* copy passages from the Bible.

An extract from a modern history book.

SOURCE B

I could not find anything bad about the convent, no matter how hard I tried. I think this was because everybody had got together and agreed to keep the convent's secrets. There were lots of relics including St Edmund's nails, St Thomas's penknife and his boots, and enough pieces of the Holy Cross to make a whole cross.

From the report on St Edmund's convent.

SOURCE C

Found the **Prior** at that time in bed with a woman, both naked, about 11 o'clock in the morning.

From the report on Crossed Friars monastery in London.

SOURCE D

The abbot delighted in playing dice and spent a lot of money on it. Women frequently came into this monastery.

From the report on St Edmund's abbey.

SOURCE E

The monks in my monastery have taken no notice of King Henry's command to cross out any mention of the Pope in all our books. The monks drink and play bowls after breakfast till ten o'clock or midday. They come to morning service drunk. They do nothing for the love of God. They have many other faults which I have no time to tell you about.

From a letter dated 1535 from Richard Beereley, a monk, to Thomas Cromwell.

SOURCE F

Henry VIII made the nobles loyal by selling property to them cheaply. He also made a lot of money from the sales. The dissolution of the monasteries gave Henry the means to stand up to the Catholic countries of Europe if they attacked him.

Adapted from *A History of Britain*, by Simon Schama, published in 2000.

Key words

Prior The monk in charge of a priory (a type of monastery).

SOURCE G

A painting showing inspectors closing down a monastery.

TASKS...

1 Copy out the table below.
  Use Sources A–G to complete the table showing the reasons why Henry VIII closed down the monasteries.

2 Source E was not written by an inspector. It was written by a monk. Does that surprise you? Do you think the monk was biased? Explain your answer.

	Source	Evidence
The monks and nuns were not following the rules of their religious houses.		
Monks and nuns still supported the Pope.		
Henry VIII needed to get the support of the nobles.		
Henry VIII needed money in case of a war against him by Catholic countries.		

What was the Pilgrimage of Grace?

Many people, especially in the north of England, protested against:

• taxes

• 'low-born' advisers to the king (they meant Thomas Cromwell)

• the closure of the monasteries.

The rebels were also angry because they had heard that some churches were to be closed. They said they were loyal to the king. They called their movement the 'Pilgrimage of Grace'.

The uprising was huge. At first Henry had to agree to talk to the rebels. He called their leader, Robert Aske, to London. Henry promised to listen to them and many rebels went home. However, Henry did not like opposition and he started to build up his army.

When he felt strong enough to strike back he invited Aske to more talks. He arrested him and executed him. Aske was hanged in chains from the walls of York Castle so that people would learn a lesson. Churches were not closed, but more monasteries were. Any monks who disobeyed Henry's orders were hanged.

What was Henry's attitude towards translating the Bible into English?

Henry was a Catholic all his life. He let the Bible be translated into English in 1539. He ordered that a copy should be placed in every church in England. But he quickly became worried. He thought that if people read the Bible they might start talking more about religion. So Henry told Parliament to pass a law to stop 'women, apprentices, serving men and labourers' from reading the Bible themselves. But it was too late. The new printing presses had already made it possible for ordinary people to own their own Bible.

💡 Why might Henry have been worried about people discussing religion?

💡 Why do you think that 'women, apprentices, serving men and labourers' were stopped from reading the Bible?

TASKS...

1 What do you think Henry VIII thought about:
   a) the Pilgrimage of Grace?
   b) religion?

2 What do you think Henry VIII thought about the English Bible?

Plenary

Which three of the five statements below do you think best sum up why Henry VIII wanted the monasteries closed?

- Henry VIII was very greedy and needed more money for his parties.

- Henry VIII needed lots of money in case he was attacked by the Catholic countries of Europe.

- Henry VIII needed to make sure the nobles of England supported him. The best way to do this was to give them land and money.

- Many monks still obeyed the Pope rather than King Henry. The king thought this was dangerous.

- Many monks were not living holy lives, but sinful ones.

Is one of the three you have chosen more important than the others? Explain your answer.

Explain your choice to a partner. Do you both agree? If you don't, try to persuade each other that you are right by using evidence to support your case.

DID ELIZABETH I FIND A 'MIDDLE WAY' IN RELIGION?

Objectives

By the end of this section you will know:
• how religion had changed by the end of Elizabeth I's reign
• why Elizabeth changed religion in England.

You will be able to:
• explain why Elizabeth's changes in religion were called a 'middle way'
• answer the big question: did England become Protestant in the sixteenth century?

Starter

Try to work out which of the following is the odd one out:

● *the Pope* ● *Martin Luther*
● *Henry VIII* ● *Robert Aske*

Discuss your choice with someone else in your class. There could be more than one correct answer.

How did Edward VI and Mary I change religion in England?

Henry VIII was a Catholic but he allowed his son, Edward, to be brought up by Protestants. Edward was only nine years old when his father died in 1547. He was too young to rule by himself. Edward's Protestant advisers started to make England a truly Protestant country.

A portrait of Edward VI as a young king.

The changes to religion in Edward VI's reign didn't affect most ordinary people. In villages people went to the same church and said the same prayers. In the larger towns much more changed.

💡 What do you think would have happened in churches to make them Protestant?

SOURCE B

A portrait of Mary I.

SOURCE C

A portrait of Elizabeth I when she first became queen in 1558.

Key words

Legitimate Born to parents who are married.

At the age of 15, Edward VI died. Henry's elder daughter, Mary Tudor, became queen. Mary I was a strict Catholic. She hated Protestant ideas and quickly put an end to her brother's changes.

💡 What do you think would have happened in churches to make them Catholic?

Mary I was 39 years old when she became Queen of England and she wanted to get a lot done quickly. She married a Catholic, Prince Philip of Spain. She began to get rid of the Protestant changes in churches. Some people were very unhappy about this and wanted the Church to stay Protestant. If people did not go back to being Catholic, she burnt them for heresy. More than 200 people may have died in this way for their beliefs.

Mary I died after only four years as queen. She had no children and her half-sister, Elizabeth, became queen. Elizabeth was the daughter of Anne Boleyn. Elizabeth reigned from 1558 until 1603.

What was Elizabeth's 'middle way' in religion?

To Catholics, Elizabeth should not have been queen. This was because, in the eyes of the Catholic Church, her mother had not been married to Henry VIII when Elizabeth was born.

Protestants, on the other hand, thought that Elizabeth was **legitimate** and the rightful queen. They did not want another Catholic monarch like Mary I. They hoped that Elizabeth would give her full backing to the Protestant Church.

But Elizabeth wanted to keep both Protestants and Catholics on her side. The Pope wanted her off the throne. She did not want to give English Catholics a reason to try to kill her.

TASKS...

1 **a)** Copy the table below. It contains the things Elizabeth did to try to get a 'middle way' in religion that would please both Protestants and Catholics. **WS**

b) Using a highlighter pen, colour all the actions which Protestants would have liked.

c) In a different colour, highlight all the actions which the Catholics would have liked.

d) If both Protestants and Catholics would have liked them, colour the actions half and half.

Have a prayer book (setting out the service) in English, written by Thomas Cranmer.	Keep all the old churches.	Have no monks.
Have a few pictures and statues in churches.	Priests to read from the English Bible in church.	Have no shrines or relics.
Don't have the Pope as Head of the Church in England.	Fines for those who refused to go to church.	The queen to be 'Supreme Governor' of the Church of England.

2 You now have enough information to be able to answer the big question at the beginning of this chapter: 'Did England become Protestant in the sixteenth century?' **WS**

Sort the following events out, putting them in the order in which they happened

• Mary I burned Protestants and made England Catholic.
• Henry VIII dissolved the monasteries.
• Henry VIII allowed people to have Bibles in English.
• Elizabeth I tried to please both Catholics and Protestants with her 'middle way' in religion.
• Edward VI's government made the English Church Protestant.
• Henry VIII broke with the Pope.

Now write three sentences about each one. Each of your sentences should answer the following questions about the event:

• Why did it happen? (What events caused it?)
• How did it happen? (Describe what happened.)
• What were the results? (Did it cause anything else to happen?)

Write a final sentence saying whether you think England was more Protestant or more Catholic by the end of Elizabeth's reign. Give some reasons for your decision.

Plenary

Which do you think was the most important of all the changes in religion in the sixteenth century? Why?

WHY WERE MARY I OF ENGLAND AND MARY, QUEEN OF SCOTS, SUCH CONTROVERSIAL FIGURES IN TUDOR ENGLAND?

WHY WERE PROTESTANTS BURNED AT THE STAKE DURING THE REIGN OF MARY I?

Objectives

In this section you are trying to decide:
- why a Protestant was killed
- who was responsible for the execution.

You will look carefully at statements to reach a conclusion.

SOURCE Ⓐ

A fictional TV detective.

Starter

- Who is the detective in Source A?
- Which other famous detectives can you think of?
- Why are the detectives you have thought of good at their job?

A historical mystery

You are now going to be a detective.

The year is 1556. A man called Thomas Wilson has been burned to death. Think back to what you learned about religious change in Chapter 1.

💡 Why do you think he was executed (killed)?

In groups, look at the statements below. Sort them into the correct order. Then answer the questions which follow. Be careful! You won't need every statement. **WS**

1   Thomas was born in 1515 when Henry VIII was king.

2   Thomas supported Henry VIII's Reformation as he believed that the king was right to become Head of the Church of England.

3   Thomas made many changes to his church. He removed any signs of the Catholic religion, including statues and pictures.

4   Thomas was delighted when Edward VI became king in 1547, as Edward was a Protestant.

5   Mary banned the new English Prayer Book. Thomas carried on using it.

6   Edward VI was always ill.

7   Mary said that the Pope was Head of the English Church. She ordered everyone to be Catholic.

8   In 1549 Thomas introduced the new English Prayer Book.

9   In 1556 Thomas was arrested for using the English Prayer Book.

10   Under torture, Thomas refused to give up his Protestant beliefs.

11   Elizabeth I was the younger daughter of Henry VIII.

12   Thomas was very upset in 1553 when he heard of Edward VI's death.

13   Mary, elder daughter of Henry VIII, became queen.

14   Mary died in 1558, lonely and unhappy.

15   The Catholics rebelled against Edward VI.

16   Thomas helped to translate the Bible into English in the early 1540s.

17   In 1538 Thomas decided on a career in the Church.

18   In 1542 Thomas became a Protestant priest.

19   Thomas was worried because Queen Mary was a Catholic.

TASKS...

1 Why was Thomas executed?

2 Who was most responsible for his death?

3 Which cards do you think were not needed?

4 Compare your findings with other groups.

Plenary

Write a letter to Thomas Wilson's mother, explaining why her son was killed.

Show your letter to someone else in your class. How different are the two letters?

DID MARY I DESERVE TO BE KNOWN AS 'BLOODY MARY'?

Objectives

In this section you will:
- look at evidence about the reign of Mary I
- decide whether she deserved to be known as 'Bloody Mary'.

SOURCE A

O Lord, Receiue my ſpirite.

The burning of a Protestant during Mary's reign. An illustration from Foxe's *Book of Martyrs*.

Starter

What is happening in Source A? What questions could you ask to find out more about what is happening? Use questions that begin 'who', 'why', 'what', 'when' and 'where'.

SOURCE B

Queen Mary believed that heretics – people who did not agree with the Catholic religion – had to be burned. This would punish them, and it would also burn away their sin. Two of the Protestants who were burned were Hugh Latimer and Nicholas Ridley. Latimer was a preacher who criticised the Catholic religion and rich people. Ridley was the Bishop of London. But the burnings did not turn people back to being Catholics. Many of those who died became **martyrs**. People started to call the queen 'Bloody Mary'. When she died in 1558, people were happy.

From a school textbook written in 1997.

Mary I and the Protestants

Look at the evidence of Sources B to I and the map on page 30.

Key words

Martyr A person who is killed for refusing to change their beliefs.

SOURCE C

A woodcut from the 1560s, showing the deaths of Bishops Latimer and Ridley.

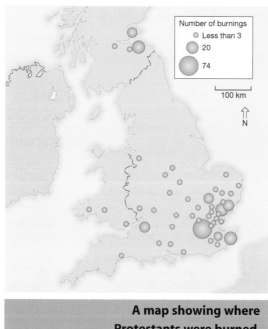

A map showing where Protestants were burned.

SOURCE D

There were 284 people burned. This included 5 bishops, 21 ministers, 8 gentlemen, 84 workers, 100 farmers, servants and labourers, 26 wives, 20 widows, 9 girls, 2 boys and 2 infants.

John Foxe, a Protestant minister, included these figures in his *Book of Martyrs*.

In 1554 Mary married Prince Philip, the son of the King of Spain. Spain was the most powerful country in Europe and it was also a Catholic country. The English were worried that Philip would tell Mary how to run England. In 1554 there was a rebellion in Kent against the wedding. Soldiers were sent to stop the rebellion and its leaders were hanged. Many Protestants opposed Mary and between 1555 and 1558 over 8300 Protestants were killed.

From a modern textbook.

SOURCE F

The Protestant Archbishop of Canterbury, Thomas Cranmer, was burned for not becoming a Catholic. An illustration from Foxe's *Book of Martyrs*.

SOURCE G

SOURCE H

A man called Rogers was burned yesterday. Some of the onlookers wept, others prayed to God to give him strength. Some gathered the ashes and the bones, others threatened the bishops. I think it would be wise to treat the Protestants better, otherwise they may rebel. Mary's Protestant sister Elizabeth has many supporters, and there are some Englishmen who don't like foreigners.

Simon Renard, a Catholic, was the Spanish Ambassador in London. He wrote this letter to Philip of Spain after watching the first Protestant being burned in 1555.

Mary I blessing rings, which were supposed to cure sickness. This picture was drawn by a Catholic in the sixteenth century.

SOURCE 1

We should not judge people in the past by our standards today. In the sixteenth century people were used to heretics being burned:

- Henry VII burned ten people.
- Henry VIII burned 81 people.
- Edward VI burned two people.
- Mary burned 284 people.
- Elizabeth burned five people.
- Every year up to 54 people were hanged in Essex for theft.
- After the Northern Rebellion in Elizabeth's reign, over 300 people were hanged.

From a modern textbook.

TASKS...

1 Find three sources that suggest that Mary deserved her nickname.

- Write down each source letter.
- Explain why you have chosen each source.

2 Find two sources that suggest she did not deserve her nickname.

- Write down each source letter.
- Explain why you have chosen each source.

3 From the evidence of the map and Sources B to I, do you think Mary deserved the nickname 'Bloody Mary'? Give a reason for your decision.

4 Think of another nickname for Mary and write this down. Explain why you have chosen this nickname.

Plenary

Write down one new word or phrase that you have learned in this chapter.

Show your word or phrase to someone else in the class. Ask them to explain what it means.

Now you could play a game of 'Taboo'. Think of a second term or word used in the chapter. Describe the word to your partner (don't use the word itself!).

WHAT DO WE KNOW OF THE LIFE AND SCANDALS OF MARY, QUEEN OF SCOTS?

Objectives

In this section you will:
- look at Mary, Queen of Scots' life and reign
- prepare a lesson on Mary Queen of Scots for younger pupils.

SOURCE A

One evening in March 1566, Mary and her ladies-in-waiting were having supper with Rizzio. Suddenly the door burst open. Darnley pushed his way in. Rizzio clung to the queen but Darnley's men dragged him away. They murdered him outside the door.

The murder of Mary, Queen of Scots' secretary, Rizzio.

Starter

Imagine you are a newspaper reporter at the scene of Rizzio's murder. Write an eye-catching headline.

The key events and scandals of Mary's life

TASKS...

1 You will read on pages 34-37 about the key events and scandals in the life of Mary, Queen of Scots, and look at source evidence. Once you have done this, in a group, prepare a lesson plan for year 5 pupils. The lesson is about the life of Mary, Queen of Scots. Include these things: **WS**

> **Starter** Something to catch their attention and interest. What about one of the murders?
> **Task** Try to get the pupils finding out something. For example, why was Darnley murdered?
> **Plenary** Give them something different but very quick to do to finish the lesson. For example, they could write down the most interesting thing they have learned.
> **Follow-up** Get them to do some extra research on something. For example, why did the people of Scotland not like Mary?

- Make the lesson as interesting and exciting as possible. You might want to make it a murder mystery. For example, did Mary, Queen of Scots order the murder of Darnley?
- What will you include? What will you leave out?
- Remember that you will have to make the information simple so the younger pupils can understand it.

The information and Sources B–H below are key events and scandals in Mary, Queen of Scots' life. Remember, your group has been asked to prepare a lesson on the life and times of Mary, Queen of Scots, for pupils in year 5.

SOURCE B

I know that the Queen regrets her marriage. She hates Darnley. Rizzio is sure to get his throat cut soon.

From a letter written by the English ambassador in Scotland, shortly before Rizzio's death.

In 1558 Mary, Queen of Scots married the eldest son of the king of France. She soon became Queen of France and Scotland. It seemed as if she was the luckiest woman in the world.

But her luck soon changed. Her husband died and she returned to Scotland in 1561.

Mary, Queen of Scots lived at Holyrood Palace in Edinburgh and ruled well. She listened to the advice of her ministers and, although she was a Catholic, she tried not to upset Scottish Protestants.

In 1565 she married Lord Darnley. She soon realised that she had made a terrible mistake. Darnley was a coward and a drunkard, unable to help her rule Scotland.

Mary, Queen of Scots, began to rely on the advice of her private secretary, Rizzio. He was an Italian. When Darnley realised that Mary preferred Rizzio, he planned to have him murdered.

Mary never forgave Darnley for Rizzio's murder.

SOURCE C

The murder of Rizzio, painted in 1833.

SOURCE D

No more tears now. I will think about revenge.

Words spoken by Mary, Queen of Scots soon after Rizzio's murder.

Mary now began to rely on the Earl of Bothwell. A few months after Rizzio's murder, an explosion blew up Darnley's house. Darnley tried to escape, but he was caught and murdered.

SOURCE E

Darnley's death is planned. If I do not kill him, I cannot live in Scotland. He will destroy me.

The Earl of Bothwell said this in 1566.

The main suspect was the Earl of Bothwell. There were rumours that Mary had planned the murder. Most people refused to believe this. Then Mary made the worst possible mistake. She married the Earl of Bothwell. He was unpopular with Protestants and Catholics.

SOURCE F

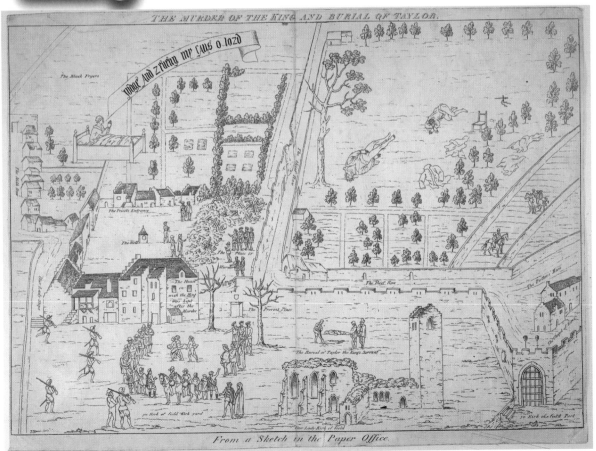

A sketch drawn at the time of Darnley's murder.

MARY I AND MARY, QUEEN OF SCOTS.

35

SOURCE G

You and I are a very good couple. Darnley troubles me. Curse him!

From a letter which Mary, Queen of Scots, wrote in 1567 to the Earl of Bothwell. Some historians think that it is a fake.

Shocked by Mary, Queen of Scots, the Scots revolted against her. The two armies – the rebels and the supporters of Mary – met at Carberry Hill. But the battle never began. When Mary saw how strong the rebel army was, she sent Bothwell away and surrendered. She was imprisoned in Loch Leven Castle.

SOURCE H

A romantic painting of the battle of Carberry Hill in 1567.

Mary, Queen of Scots managed to escape with the help of one of her servants. She was rowed across the loch to where friends were waiting to meet her. Mary raised a new army, but it was defeated at the battle of Langside.

Mary escaped and fled to England. She asked her cousin, the Protestant Queen Elizabeth I of England, to protect her.

Queen Elizabeth allowed Mary, Queen of Scots to stay in England. She was kept as a prisoner because Elizabeth was worried Mary might try to claim the English throne. For 19 years Mary, Queen of Scots was kept in different castles, including Sheffield, Bolton, Wakefield, and Tutbury.

Plenary
Check your lesson plan. Have you missed out any important details?

WHAT SHOULD BE DONE ABOUT MARY, QUEEN OF SCOTS?

Objectives

In this section you will:

• look at the problems Elizabeth I had with Mary, Queen of Scots.

You will try to decide:

• Was Elizabeth I right to order Mary, Queen of Scots' execution?
• Was Mary, Queen of Scots guilty?

Dear Agony Aunt

I need your advice. I think my cousin is plotting to kill me. What should I do?

Elizabeth I

Starter

Jot down a quick reply to this letter. Share it with others in the class. Now read the description of Mary's execution in Source A. Think of two key words to describe the execution. Share them with others in the class.

💡 *Think of three key words to describe the execution. Share these with someone else in your class.*

Mary took off her cloak as she moved towards the block. The crowd gazed at her bright scarlet dress. She stepped forward and prayed aloud as she knelt down. It took three blows of the axe to remove her head. After the first blow Mary made no noise. After the third blow the executioner grasped her wig to hold up her head for everyone to see. People were shocked to see Mary's grey hair as her head fell to the ground. After all, she was only 45 years old. A small, scared dog ran from underneath Mary's skirts, but it would not leave her. When Elizabeth heard of the execution she was shocked. She had not meant this to happen.

A description of Mary, Queen of Scots' execution, from a modern textbook.

Was Mary guilty of treason? The evidence

As you read through the pieces of evidence against Mary, give each one a rating from 1 to 5 for how guilty each one shows Mary to be:

1 = Not Mary's idea – not guilty.

5 = Mary is totally involved – guilty.

I support your wish to prevent our enemies from destroying the Catholic religion in England. The longer we delay, the stronger our enemies will become. Once everything is prepared and our forces are ready, I must be rescued from here to wait for foreign help.

Mary, Queen of Scots' letter to Babington.

The Babington Plot, 1586

Babington and other Catholics planned to rebel, kill Queen Elizabeth and put Mary, Queen of Scots, on the throne. Babington wrote to Mary, Queen of Scots who replied, in code, agreeing to the plot. The letters were hidden in beer barrels and smuggled in and out of the castle. Elizabeth's spies cracked the code and she now had the evidence she needed to execute Mary.

The Throckmorton Plot, 1583

Throckmorton was a Catholic who took letters from Mary, Queen of Scots to the Spanish Ambassador. Throckmorton wanted to rebel with help from Spain.

Again, Elizabeth's spies found out and Throckmorton and others were executed.

Philip of Spain

Mary, Queen of Scots was Catholic, and so was Spain and its king, Philip. Relations with Spain grew tense in the 1580s, when Protestant Elizabeth was on the throne.

Elizabeth suspected that Mary, Queen of Scots might ask Catholic Spain for help.

The Ridolfi Plot, 1571

This was a plot to overthrow Elizabeth. The plotters wanted Mary, Queen of Scots to marry the Duke of Norfolk, who was the leading Catholic English noble. They wanted to place Mary, Queen of Scots on the throne.

The plotters were to be helped by the Pope and the king of Spain, but Elizabeth's spies found out about the plot. Norfolk was executed.

SOURCE C

Sir Francis Walsingham.

Sir Francis Walsingham

He was the head of Elizabeth's secret service. He had more than 70 spies in towns and ports in Europe. These spies sent him news of Catholic plots against Elizabeth.

His spies found the letter that Mary, Queen of Scots wrote to Babington. Some historians think that Walsingham was out to get Mary and could have made up the evidence.

The Northern Rebellion, 1569

Many people in the north of England were still Catholic at heart, even though England was Protestant.

The plan was to seize Mary, Queen of Scots, march to London and force Elizabeth to return to the Catholic religion.

Elizabeth sent her troops, who defeated the rebels and hanged 800 of them.

TASKS...

1 Do you think Mary, Queen of Scots was guilty of plotting against Queen Elizabeth?

a) Find two reasons to prove her guilt. Share these with someone else in your class. Do they have the same reasons?

b) Find one reason to show Mary was not guilty. Share it with someone else in your class. Do they have the same evidence?

2 What should Elizabeth do? Below are her choices:

Choice 1:

Hand Mary back to the Scots who might execute her for murder. Elizabeth is horrified at the thought of executing a queen, and Mary is her cousin.

Choice 3:

Keep Mary in prison forever. Elizabeth will not have to kill her own cousin. But this will leave Mary at the centre of plots to overthrow Elizabeth.

Choice 2:

Allow Mary to be free in England. Mary might attract friends, especially nobles who do not like Elizabeth, and lead a revolt against her. After all, Mary is attractive and has already had three husbands.

Choice 4:

Execute Mary. Elizabeth has evidence that Mary has taken part in Babington's plan to murder her. She could set up a court to try Mary and, if she is guilty, have her executed. However, this means that she has to order the death of a queen who is also her own cousin.

a) In groups, decide what Elizabeth should do.
b) Why did you make this choice?
c) Now write a diary entry for Queen Elizabeth in which she explains:
  • the choices she had
  • her difficulties in making the decision
  • what she finally decided, and why.

> What should I do about my cousin Mary, Queen of Scots?
>
> I have four choices. These are: ...
>
> I find making a decision difficult because ...
>
> I have made the following choice ...
>
> This is because ...

A drawing of the execution of Mary, Queen of Scots. Servants are shown outside burning her clothes.

Plenary

Elizabeth decided to have Mary, Queen of Scots executed in 1587. Did she make the right choice?

Now that you have read the evidence, write a detailed reply to the Agony Aunt letter on page 38. Compare answers with someone else in your class.

WHY WERE ENGLISH PEOPLE FIGHTING EACH OTHER IN THE SEVENTEENTH CENTURY?

WHO OR WHAT CAUSED THE CIVIL WAR?

Objectives

In this section you will try to understand:
- the reasons for the Civil War
- who or what was most to blame for the Civil War.

Starter

Civil War breaks out after Queen and Prime Minister row!

Queen Gertrude has stopped the Prime Minister banning football. The Prime Minister says that by doing this, the Queen has taken his powers. The Queen argues that she still has the power to stop laws which she believes are against the people.

This is a made-up story which is unlikely to happen. If it did happen, though, which side would you support? Why? Does the person sitting next to you share your views?

In 1625, Charles I became king of England. During his reign, Britain had a **Civil War**. The war had many causes. They included:

- the great changes taking place in England in the sixteenth and seventeenth centuries

- arguments between the king and Parliament.

What happened during the Civil War?

The people of England were divided. The king's supporters called **Cavaliers** or Royalists fought Parliament's supporters called **Roundheads**. Fathers, mothers, sons and daughters supported different sides.

The Civil War lasted from 1642 to 1649. The Roundheads (Parliament) won. Did they win because they were strong or because the Royalists were weak?

In 1649, Charles I was tried by Parliament, found guilty and executed. Should the king have been killed? Was he guilty of **treason**?

From 1649 to 1660, England was not ruled by a king or queen. Instead, it was controlled by the leader of Parliament, Oliver Cromwell, until he died in 1658.

In 1660, Charles II was made king. England was a **monarchy** once more.

Key words

Civil war A war between two or more groups of people in the same country.

Cavaliers Nickname given to the king's supporters.

Roundheads Nickname given to Parliament's supporters.

Treason Betraying your country.

Monarchy When a king, queen, emperor or empress rules a country.

TASKS...

1 Read the information and sources A-G below.

2 As you read, jot down as many reasons as you can find to explain why Parliament fell out with the king.

Key words

Puritans Protestants who wanted simple church services.

What happened in the years before the Civil War?

Great changes were taking place which led to arguments between the king and his Parliament.

A growing number of middle-class people wanted a say in how England was run.

At the same time, the powers of the monarch had increased under Henry VIII and Elizabeth I.

By the time Charles I became king in 1625, many **Puritans** had become MPs. They wanted religion to be simple. They wanted a bigger say in how the country was run and less power for the king.

Charles I's father, James I, believed in the 'Divine Right of Kings'. He believed that kings were given their power to rule by God and so they must therefore be obeyed. Charles I shared this belief.

💡 What reasons can you see so far for Charles I and Parliament to argue?

A painting of Charles I with the crown, orb and sceptre.

The reign of Charles I

Charles I started badly. He married a Catholic. Parliament was worried that she might make Charles a Catholic too.

Parliament and the Petition of Right

Shortly after Charles became king, England went to war with Austria and France. Charles was very short of money. He made rich people lend him some. But it was not enough.

In 1628, Charles asked Parliament for more money. He wanted Parliament to raise special taxes on goods, called **customs duties**. Angry MPs presented Charles with the Petition of Right (see Source B on page 46).

Key words

Customs duties Taxes that are added to the price of goods which are imported into a country.

It is said by a law of King Edward I that there should be no taxes without Parliament's agreement. In the reign of King Edward III it was said that no person should be made to make any loans to the king. Yet some people have been asked to lend money to King Charles I. When they have refused some of them have been put in prison without trial.

From the Petition of Right, written in 1628.

Parliament asked the king to stop making people lend him money and putting people in prison without trial. Charles agreed, but when MPs gave him an increase in customs duties for only one year, he dismissed Parliament. From 1629, Charles ruled for 11 years without Parliament. This time is called the period of 'personal rule'.

Religious changes

In 1633 William Laud became Archbishop of Canterbury. He was a Protestant but he did not like Puritans and thought they had too much influence on the Church of England. He brought back stained-glass windows and special clothes for priests. Many Puritans were angry. They believed he was making the Church of England too much like the Catholic Church again.

Four years later, Charles tried to make the Scots use the new English Prayer Book. They refused because most Scots were **Presbyterian**. In 1639 the king sent an army to force the Scots to agree. The Scots defeated the English army.

Key words

Presbyterian Protestants who believe that the Church should be run in a different way.

SOURCE C

The Arch-Prelate of St Andrewes in Scotland reading the new Service-booke in his pontificalibus assaulted by men & Women, with Cricketts stooles Stickes and Stones.

An engraving showing Scots rioting against the English Prayer Book in 1637.

Charles had no money to raise a second army to send to Scotland, so he recalled Parliament in 1639 to ask for more money. The MPs refused and Charles dismissed Parliament.

Charles' second army was defeated by the Scots. In 1640 Charles was forced to call Parliament again to ask for a **grant**. This time Parliament was determined to reduce the king's powers.

SOURCE D

I shall explain to you the problems in this country …
Firstly, Parliament was dismissed before our complaints were heard. Several men were put in prison for saying what they believed.
Secondly, there have been changes in religion … the introduction of Catholic ceremonies and the like.
Thirdly, there is the taking of taxes without Parliament's agreement.

A speech made by the MP John Pym in April 1640.

Key words

Grant A gift of money requiring official approval.

Rebellion in Ireland

In 1641 there was rebellion in Ireland. Irish Catholics, fearing the English Parliament would pass anti-Catholic laws, killed 3000 Protestants (see Source E). Charles needed money for an army to put down the Irish rebels. He had to recall Parliament.

The MPs were led by the Puritan John Pym. They said that Parliament should decide who led this army. The king would not agree.

Driuinge Men Women & children by hund: reds vpon Briges & casting them into Riuers, who drowned not were killed with poles & shot with muskets.

G

A drawing showing Catholics killing Protestants in Ireland in 1641.

Parliament opposes the king

Parliament forced Charles to get rid of the Earl of Strafford, his chief minister, and Archbishop Laud. Both men were hated for carrying out the wishes of Charles I. Strafford was executed in 1641 and Laud was put in prison.

In November 1641, Pym gave Parliament a long list of what the king had done wrong. This was known as the Grand Remonstrance.

Charles was furious. He was determined to show who ruled the country. On 4 January he went to the House of Commons to arrest Pym and four other rebel MPs. The five MPs escaped by boat down the River Thames. Many people were shocked by these actions. By law, MPs could not be arrested when they were in the House of Commons.

A painting, done in the nineteenth century showing the five MPs escaping by boat.

Tuesday, 4 January 1642.

The King came with his soldiers. He told us that the five MPs were guilty of treason. He asked the Speaker if the five were in the House. The Speaker fell on his knees and said he had neither eyes, nor tongue, to see or say anything but what the MPs told him. Then the King said he thought his own eyes were good and that the MPs were gone.

Sir Ralph Verney, an MP, describes what happened when the king entered the House of Commons.

TASKS...

Work in groups.

1 Make a list of as many reasons as you can think of for Parliament and the king falling out.

2 **a)** Now, using a red highlighter pen, mark those reasons for which the king was most to blame.

b) With a blue highlighter pen, mark those reasons for which Parliament was most to blame.

c) Use a yellow highlighter pen to show those reasons for which both sides were to blame.

3 Draw a line, like the one below, and decide where you would put Charles I or Parliament.

●━━━━━━━━━━━━━━━━━━━━━━━━━━●

To blame   Not to blame

4 Compare your line with other groups' decisions.

   a) Are they different?

   b) Why are they different?

   c) Was any group on the king's side?

5 In less than 100 words, explain who or what you think caused the Civil War. Here is a writing frame to help you.

> I believe Charles I caused the Civil War because …
>
> I believe Parliament was also to blame because …
>
> I think that most to blame was …
>
> This is because …

Plenary

Discuss in your group how you came to your conclusions about who or what caused the Civil War.

WHY WAS KING CHARLES I DEFEATED?

Objectives

In this section you will:
• work out reasons for the defeat of Charles I.

SOURCE Ⓐ

This picture was drawn by a Parliamentarian. It shows the murder of women and children by Royalists in 1644.

SOURCE Ⓑ

A Royalist newspaper shows the attacks carried out by Parliament's army.

Starter

What are Sources A and B trying to show about the other side in the Civil War? Why do you think they are showing them like this?

Sources A and B are examples of propaganda. Propaganda gives only one view of an event or person. It is often used in war. Source C is an example of propaganda used during the First World War by America against Germany.

SOURCE Ⓒ

Propaganda used during the First World War.
The 'mad brute' is Germany.

WHY WERE ENGLISH PEOPLE FIGHTING EACH OTHER?

💡 *How do you think propaganda might be used? Tell your ideas to a partner and see what they think.*

💡 *Why do both sides in a war use propaganda?*

TIMELINE OF THE CIVIL WAR 1642–9

1642   Battle of Edgehill ends in a draw.

1643   Royalist army fails to reach London.
Royalist army captures Bristol.
Cromwell trains his New Model Army.

1644   The Scots join the Civil War on Parliament's side.
Parliament's army defeats Prince Rupert and the Royalists at the Battle of Marston Moor.

1645   New Model Army fights on Parliament's side.
Battle of Naseby.

1646   Parliament captures Oxford from Charles I.

1648   Cromwell defeats Charles.

1649   Charles is arrested and put on trial.

The Civil War, 1642–9

💡 As you read about the Civil War, jot down reasons for Charles I's defeat using a spider diagram.

Oliver Cromwell and the New Model Army

Oliver Cromwell was an MP and a Puritan. He had been angry with Charles I's refusal to give in to Parliament's demands (see pages 48-9).

Cromwell was a very good soldier. Between 1644 and 1645, he set up the New Model Army – an army to fight for Parliament against the king. Before this time there had been no national army. Cromwell picked only men who supported Parliament. They were very well trained.

Cromwell took great care of his soldiers. He made sure that they were paid well. In return, they were expected to behave well. They were also religious men, believing they were doing God's will.

A modern artist's impression of the New Model Army.

Key battles of the Civil War

Battle of Edgehill, October 1642

This was the first big battle of the Civil War. The king's nephew, Prince Rupert, led the Royalist **cavalry**. He was young and inexperienced. The Royalists attacked the Roundheads. Each side fought until they were exhausted. Neither side won, but the battle stopped Charles from capturing London, England's most important city.

Battle of Marston Moor, July 1644

Prince Rupert fought against Parliament's army at Marston Moor. He made a big mistake. Rupert thought that the enemy was not ready. He was starting to eat supper when Parliament's army attacked.
The Royalists lost the battle and the king lost control of the north of England.

Key words

Cavalry Soldiers on horseback.

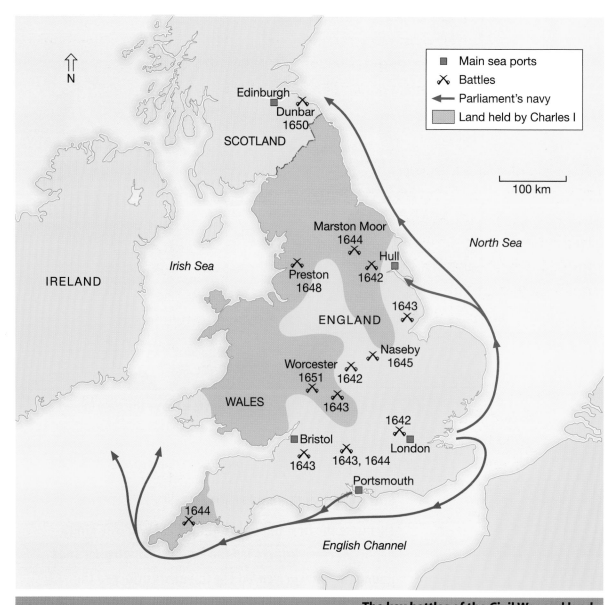

The key battles of the Civil War and land held by King Charles and Parliament.

Battle of Naseby, June 1645

The Royalists faced the New Model Army for the first time. The Royalist army was no match for Cromwell's men. This was the last major battle of the war. The king had lost.

Why was Charles I defeated?

Charles made several mistakes during the Civil War. Parliament also had strengths. Below are statements which are a mix of Charles' mistakes and Parliament's strengths:

The king had rich supporters, but they ran out of money. At Naseby, the king's soldiers were badly equipped compared to the New Model Army. After this he might have got another army, but he had no money to pay the soldiers.

Parliament controlled the south east of England, which was the richest part of the country, and so had the money to pay for the war.

Parliament chose very good leaders such as Oliver Cromwell and Sir Thomas Fairfax.

Charles placed the inexperienced Prince Rupert in charge of his armies.

The navy was on the side of Parliament. This made it easier to get men and supplies from abroad.

Charles left London at the start of the Civil War, which meant that Parliament controlled the most important city. In 1643 Charles tried unsuccessfully to capture London.

Parliament got the support of the Scots by promising that it would set up a Presbyterian Church in England like the one in Scotland. In return, an army of 20,000 Scots joined the Parliamentarians and defeated the Royalists at Marston Moor.

TASKS...

Why was Charles I defeated? Work in groups.

1 Look at your spider diagram showing the reasons for Charles I's defeat in the Civil War.

a) Organise your reasons under these headings:
- Parliament's strengths
- The king's weaknesses

b) Now decide how important each reason was for the defeat of Charles I. Use a scale of 1 to 5. If you think the reason was important, give it a rating of 5. If you think the reason was not important at all, give it a rating of 1.

2 On a sheet of A3 paper make a concept map showing the reasons for the defeat of Charles. Below is an example of a concept map showing the causes of the Civil War to help you.

3 On your own, write an answer to the following question:

Why was Charles I defeated in the Civil War? **WS**

| Attitude of Parliament | Religious change | Economic change | Growth of trade led to emergence of middle class | Social change |

Parliament wanted more say in how the country was ruled. This clashed with Charles' view on the divine right of kings

Reasons for the Civil War

Attitude of Charles I

Both believed in the divine right of kings

| Charles I ruled without Parliament | Conflicts between Charles I and Parliament | Charles I tried to arrest four members of Parliament | Attitude of James I |

Plenary

In groups, read the following description of the Civil War. See how many mistakes you can find. **WS**

The English Civil War by Professor Botchit

The Civil War broke out in 1643, with the first battle at Edgehill. Here the New Model Army fought against the Royalists led by Prince Rupert. Neither side won, but it did stop Parliament from capturing London.

Two years later, the two armies met at Marston Moor. This time the Royalists won because of a fast attack by the cavalry led by Prince Rupert. The king kept control of the north of England.

The final big battle was at Naseby in 1847. The Royalists were defeated and Charles had lost the war.

The Irish fought on Parliament's side and Charles won the support of the Scots. Parliament won because Richard Cromwell had set up the New Model Army before the war started. One of its leaders was George Fairfax.

Once you have spotted all the mistakes, write out the description with all of the mistakes corrected.

WAS CHARLES I A TRAITOR?

Objectives

In this section you will:
- decide whether Charles I was a **traitor**.

Starter

Write out three questions that you would like to ask about Source A. As you work through this section, see if you can answer these questions.

SOURCE A

The execution of Charles I in 1649, painted at the time.

The trial and execution of Charles I

In 1649, Charles I was arrested and put on trial. He was tried in a special court set up by Parliament. He was accused of being a **tyrant**, and of causing the deaths of many people during the Civil War.

Key words

Traitor A person who betrays their country.
Tyrant An evil ruler.

There were meant to be 135 judges at the trial, but only 85 turned up. Some were too frightened to come. Others disagreed with the trial.

- Name a present-day tyrant.
- Why do you think this person is a tyrant?

I believe in people's freedom as much as anybody … but I must tell you that their freedom means having a government. It is not having a share in government … that is nothing to do with them. An ordinary person and a king are two different things … If I had given way … I need not have come here. I am a martyr of the people …

Charles I's last speech.

The soldiers believed that God had already passed sentence on Charles in battle. His defeats were a sign that God was against him.

From a modern history textbook.

Although Charles I was a shy man, he talked well at his trial. He refused to answer the charges made against him. He said that the court was not a proper court and did not have the power to try him.

But 59 of the judges found him guilty and the court sentenced:

'Charles Stuart, as a Tyrant, Traitor and Murderer and public enemy to be put to death.'

Charles was executed on 30 January 1649 at Whitehall in London. He made a short speech and then laid his head on the block. There was said to have been a great groan from the crowd as his head was cut off.

Now look at the following evidence from the trial and execution of Charles I.

Charles is a tyrant. He rules according to his will rather than the law.

Life won't be the same if the king is gone. I know most people are against the execution.

If Charles is executed it will be the army's doing, not the people's.

Charles wasted tax-payers money. Why should a king get away with such things?

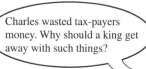

Parliament promises peace in England. I say end the wars that Charles started!

Charles tried to take away the freedom of the people. He has to be stopped.

No-one has the right to deny the divine right of kings.

A cartoon showing arguments about what to do with Charles in 1649.

SOURCE D

Charles, King of England, had wickedly tried to create for himself total power to rule and to overthrow the rights and freedom of the people. To do this, he fought a war against Parliament and the people. He is responsible for all the killings and damage caused by the war. He is therefore a TYRANT, traitor and murderer.

The charges against Charles I at his trial.

SOURCE E

The trial of Charles I in 1649.

TASKS...

1 Look at the cartoon illustration on page 58 and Sources B, C and D.
   a) Which sources suggest that Charles I was guilty?
   b) Why do they say he was guilty?

2 **a)** Are there any sources which show Charles I to be innocent?
   b) Which are they?
   c) Why do they say he was innocent?

3 Now, write your own answer to the question:
   Was Charles I guilty of treason?
   Use information from the sources and what you know about Charles I and the Civil War.

4 Prepare speeches for the trial of Charles I. Imagine you are either:
   • Charles' lawyer (the defence lawyer). Use Source B. Charles is trying to prove he is not guilty.
   or
   • Parliament's lawyer (the prosecution). Use Sources C and D. Parliament is trying to prove Charles is guilty so they can kill him.

Plenary

Do you think Parliament had the right to kill the king? What else could they have done? Could you imagine this happening in Britain today? Explain why.

HOW MUCH DID ENGLAND CHANGE AS A RESULT OF THE CIVIL WAR?

Objectives

In this section you will look at:

- how much change there was in England after the Civil War
- how much things stayed the same (**continuity**)
- why there are so many different views about Cromwell.

Key words

Continuity Things staying the same or hardly changing.

Starter

Sir Hugo Ponsonby-Smythe was a Royalist. Some of the events described below would have pleased him, others would have made him unhappy.

1 In 1642 Charles I marched into Parliament to arrest five MPs. All five escaped.	2 The Royalist army lost the Battle of Marston Moor in 1644.
3 In 1644 the Royalists held off attacks by Parliament's soldiers in the south and west of England.	4 In 1645 the Royalist army lost the Battle of Naseby.
5 In 1647 Charles was put in prison by Parliament.	6 In 1648 Charles escaped from prison. In secret, he arranged for a Scottish army to march into England on his side.
7 In 1649 Charles was put on trial and found guilty of treason.	8 In 1649 Charles was executed.

Plot Sir Hugo's reactions to events on a living graph like the one below. Compare your living graph with others in your class. Are there any differences? What are they? **WS**

TASKS...

1 As you read through the information below, draw two spider diagrams showing:

- the changes that took place between 1649 and 1660

- the things that stayed the same in that time.

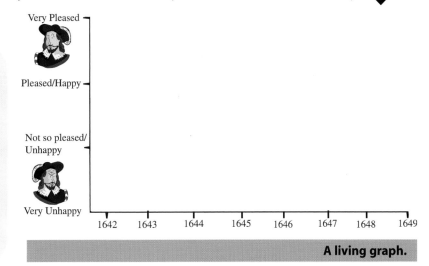

A living graph.

What happened between 1649 and 1660?

Quarrels in Parliament

There were many quarrels between Parliament and the army's leaders between 1649 and 1653. In 1653, an angry Oliver Cromwell turned MPs out of Parliament by force.

The army's leaders tried to find a new system of ruling the country. They made Cromwell a ruler for life, naming him Lord Protector instead of king. Cromwell did call some Parliaments but none of them pleased him, so he kept power to himself.

Problems in Ireland

In 1649 Cromwell went to Ireland to stop a Catholic revolt. He destroyed the Drogheda **garrison** and killed 3,500 people. His treatment of the Irish was very harsh to prevent them rebelling again.

Key words

Garrison A military camp where troops are stationed.
Levellers Puritans who thought that all men were equal and should share power.

The Levellers

In May 1649 Cromwell captured 340 **Levellers**. The Levellers were a group that wanted to change the way the country was governed. This made them a threat to Cromwell.

WHY WERE ENGLISH PEOPLE FIGHTING EACH OTHER?

Cromwell locked the Levellers up in a church and forced them to watch as three Leveller soldiers were shot dead. (You will read more about the Levellers on pages 73-6).

Puritan ideals

Cromwell's government saw itself as protector of the Puritans. People had to live a Puritan lifestyle. No gambling or drunkenness was allowed. Sport was banned. Theatres were closed and it was forbidden to celebrate Christmas. But although everyone had to live in the Puritan way, they did not have to become Puritans.

Under Cromwell, taxes on the rich went up and the money was given to the poor. The poor were treated better at this time.

Cromwell also made sure that newspapers were **censored**, so that they only printed what he allowed them to print.

Key words

Censored Checked by authorities and altered to suit them.

Cromwell died in 1658. For a short time Richard, his son, ruled as Lord Protector. In 1659 Richard resigned and in the following year Charles II was made king.

TASKS...

1 **a)** On your spider diagram, shade each of the factors you have identified in a different colour depending on whether they are:
   - political – to do with government and who ruled (in green)
   - religious (in red)
   - social (in blue).
   b) Which factor saw the most change?

c) Which factor saw the least change?

2 Think about the changes that took place in England from 1649 to 1660. Were they good or bad for England? Explain your answer.

3 Explain if you think Oliver Cromwell was a better ruler than
   a) Charles I
   b) Henry VIII.

Different interpretations of Cromwell

Oliver Cromwell's body was dug up three years after his death and beheaded.

Look at Source A.

💡 Why do you think that there is a spike through Cromwell's skull?

💡 Who do you think did this and when?

💡 What does this tell you about people's feelings towards Cromwell?

💡 Can you remember what happened to other 'traitors' before Cromwell?

There have been many different views of Oliver Cromwell, both at the time and from later historians. These views are usually about the events described in Sources B–E.

💡 As you read Sources B-E about Cromwell, decide which are:

- on Cromwell's side
- against him
- neither for nor against him.

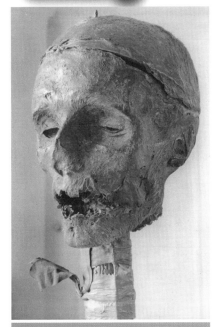

Cromwell's skull on a spike.

Cromwell is so wicked that he will end up in hell. Yet he has some qualities and he will be looked upon by people in years to come as a brave bad man.

Lord Clarendon supported Charles I and became chief minister under Charles II in the 1660s.

You … the person who brought us freedom … have achieved more things than our kings … You have taken upon yourself … to rule three powerful nations … to lead their peoples to a better standard of life.

The writer and poet, John Milton, who served in Cromwell's government.

Oliver Cromwell died hated by all except a few close friends. It is only in the last hundred years that he has been given the honour due to him in English history. He was successful in his wars abroad and was able to defeat the rebellion in Ireland. At home he gave the English people peace and order.

A historian writing in 1952.

WHY WERE ENGLISH PEOPLE FIGHTING EACH OTHER?

In the nineteenth century as Parliament became more important in helping rule the country, historians were more sympathetic towards Cromwell. Yet here was the man who crushed rebellion in Ireland, supported Charles I's execution, ordered the killing of the leading Levellers and, above all else, banned football and Christmas.

An extract from a modern history textbook, written in 1996.

TASKS...

1 Make a copy of the table below in your book.

Source	On the side of Cromwell	Against Cromwell	Neither for nor against	Reason for interpretation
A				
B				
C				
D				
E				

   a) Use the information in the sources to fill it in.

   b) Briefly explain each of your choices. For example, pick out certain words or facts given in the source.

2 Now write your own view or interpretation of Cromwell in no more than 50 words. You can do this in the form of an obituary (a person's life story, written after they have died).

Plenary

Imagine Oliver Cromwell was alive today. You might like to ask him some questions. Pretend you are going to do a TV interview with him. Write a list of questions you would ask Oliver Cromwell.

HOW FAR DID THE PURITANS CHANGE LIFE IN ENGLAND IN THE LATE 1640s AND EARLY 1650s?

WHAT DID IT MEAN TO BE A PURITAN?

Objectives

By the end of this section you will:
- know that Puritans wanted people to live 'godly' lives
- understand what was thought to be 'godly' and 'ungodly'.

Starter
From the work you have already done on religion, try to remember two things which made Protestants different from Catholics. Swap your ideas with someone else in your class and try to remember theirs as well as yours. If their ideas are the same, try to think of a different idea to add to your list. Then swap all the ideas you have with another member of the class. Do this until you have six different things which show the differences between Catholics and Protestants.

Why did people think differently about religion after the Civil War?

After the Civil War ended in 1649 some big changes took place in people's lives.

- At the end of the Civil War King Charles I had been executed

- For a while, Puritans ran the country

- They tried to control religion as well as the government

- They made a lot of changes to how people lived

What did Puritans believe?

The Puritans wanted the Church to be purer and more simple. They thought everyone should live very 'godly' lives. This meant they should dress simply and try to be good. They should read the Bible and pray a lot.

💡 If you wanted to make people live more 'godly' lives, what things would you change? For example, would you stop all gambling? The National Lottery gives a lot of money to charities. Where would they get their money from if this stopped?

TASKS...

1 In pairs, brainstorm what you think a 'godly' life' means. (Think about how you behave and what things you do that you shouldn't.)

2 You are going to collect information about how Puritans believed people should live their lives. As you read through this section, write your findings in a table like the one below.

Things people should do (how to live a godly life)	Things people shouldn't do (what makes a sinful life)

Making England 'free of sin'

Once in charge of running the country, the Puritans wanted to make England a place 'free of sin'. They began to make laws banning 'sinful' things. Fun and games were 'out'. Prayer, Bible-reading and good deeds were 'in'.

A seventeenth-century illustration showing a Puritan family at mealtime.

This picture shows Puritan ideas about sinful activities which should not be seen on a Sunday and the ways in which godly people should spend their Sundays.

TASKS...

1 a) How is the family meal in Source A different from your meals at home? Write down as many differences as you can. Compare your list with someone else.

b) Which meal do you think you would like best? Why?

c) Why do you think Puritans would eat their meals like this?

2 Look at Source B. On one side it shows what Puritans thought people should do on a Sunday. On the other side it shows what they thought people shouldn't do. See how many of each you can list.

TASKS...

3 Now, decide whether the following activities should be classed as wrong to do on Sundays or things which should be done on Sundays. Add them to your table:

Horse-racing	Cock-fighting
Giving a sermon at dinner	Going to the theatre
Giving presents to the elderly	Gambling
Drinking alcohol in a pub	Dancing
Going for a walk	Walking to church
Doing the housework	Mending clothes
Celebrating Christmas	

SOURCE C

Friday *the Four and twentieth day of* December, 1652.

Resolved by the Parliament,

That the Markets be kept to Morrow, being the Five and twentieth day of *December*; And that the Lord Major, and Sheriffs of *London* and *Middlesex*, and the Justices of Peace for the City of *Westminster* and Liberties thereof, do take care, That all such persons as shall open their Shops on that day, be protected from Wrong or Violence, and the Offenders punished.

Resolved by the Parliament,

That no Observation shall be had of the Five and twentieth day of *December*, commonly called *Christmas-Day*; nor any Solemnity used or exercised in Churches upon that Day in respect thereof.

Ordered by the Parliament,

That the Lord Major of the City of *London*, and Sheriffs of *London* and *Middlesex*, and the Justices of Peace of *Middlesex* respectively, be Authorized and Required to see this Order duly observed within the late Lines of Communication, and weekly Bills of Mortality.

Hen: Scobell, Cleric. Parliamenti.

London, Printed by *John Field*, Printer to the Parliament of *England*. 1652.

The 1652 law banning the celebration of Christmas.

Christmas is forbidden
In 1652 Parliament decided that it was 'ungodly' to celebrate Christmas. You can see from Source D on page 69 that some people felt that this was going too far.

SOURCE D

The Vindication of
CHRISTMAS,
OR,
His Twelve Yeares Observations upon the Times, concerning the lamentable Game called Sweep-stake ; acted by General *Plunder*, and Major General *Tax*; With his Exhortation to the people ; a description of that oppressing Ringworm called *Excise* ; and the manner how our high and mighty Christmas-Ale that formerly would knock down *Hercules*, & trip up the heels of a Giant, strook into a deep Consumption with a blow from *Westminster*.

> Keep out, you come not here,

> O Sir, I bring good cheere.

> Old Christmas welcome ; Do not fear.

Nr: 22 Imprinted at London for G. Horton, 1653.

A drawing called the 'Vindication of Christmas', which was produced in 1653. 'Vindication' is when something is defended.

TASKS...

1 Working in groups, discuss the following questions. Use what you have learnt about the Puritans to help you:

a) Why do you think Parliament tried to stop people celebrating Christmas?

b) What do you think people would have said when soldiers came round on Christmas day and took their dinner out of the oven?

c) Do you think that people stopped celebrating Christmas? Why?

Plenary

The Puritans tried lots of ways to make people live more godly lives. Write down three things they did which you think would have been successful and three things you think would not have worked. Explain why you have picked each one.

WHY WERE THERE SO MANY DIFFERENT RELIGIOUS GROUPS AT THIS TIME? WHAT DID THEY BELIEVE?

Objectives

By the end of this section you will:
- know that many different religious groups sprang up after the Civil War
- understand some of the differences between the various groups.

SOURCE A

THE
World turn'd upfide down:
OR,
A briefe defcription of the ridiculous Fafhions of thefe diftracted Times.

By T.J. a well-willer to King, Parliament and Kingdom.

London : Printed for *John Smith.* 1647.
Jan: 26

Starter

💡 *What things can you think of that had been 'turned upside down' by the Civil War? Make a list. Why have you chosen each of them?*

This was how one person saw the changes the Civil War brought to people's lives.

Why did so many different religious groups appear during and after the Civil War?

Many people read the Bible to help them in the 1650s. Some people believed that the Bible had the answers to all of life's problems. But the Bible is a very big book and different people found different answers in it.

💡 Where can we go to today to find the 'answers to all of life's problems'. Who can we talk to? Which of these ways existed in the seventeenth century?

A lot of different people decided that they knew best what the Bible said. This led to some strange events. Several pregnant women claimed to be about to give birth to a new Saviour (a new Jesus). A lot of people thought Christ was about to come to Earth again. A man called James Nayler rode into Bristol on a donkey just like Jesus had done in the Holy Land. Women laid palms in his path - just like when Jesus entered Jerusalem. Nayler was punished very harshly.

What were the different religious groups?

After the Civil War lots of different religious groups sprang up. Some, like the Baptists and The Society of Friends, still exist. Others, like the Aposticals, Fifth Monarchists and Familists, did not last very long. Cromwell's Puritan government was worried by some of the groups. Look back at the previous section to help you understand why.

The Anabaptists (or Baptists) believed that people should be 'born again' like Jesus when he was baptised by John the Baptist. Baptists tried to set up their own villages and sometimes defended their beliefs with violence.

Adamites believed in getting back to nature like the first human beings - Adam and Eve. Unlike other people at the time, they did not think that the human body should be kept hidden.

Familists thought that heaven and hell were real places and could be found in this world. They based their religion on love and the family.

Seekers were looking for the perfect religion and so tried lots of different ones. But they didn't like any of them.

The Society of Friends thought that the spirit of love would inspire people. There was no need for organised church services. At their meetings they waited for inspiration and often went into a trance, shaking with emotion. This led to their nickname - Quakers.

The Ranters said that people who had been chosen by God could not sin, so it was all right to behave in any way they wished. They shocked people with their ideas about free love, drinking, smoking and swearing.

The Fifth Monarchists believed that there had been four kingdoms in history and that the execution of Charles I in 1649 was the start of the Fifth Monarchy. Now the **Messiah** would come to earth again and rule over people. They thought that Cromwell was acting like a king which was wrong.

Key words

Messiah A hoped-for leader of a religious cause, like Jesus.

 Which of these religious groups do you think the government would have liked? Why did you choose these?

 Which groups would it not have liked? Why do you think this?

SOURCE B

A print from 1644 showing some of the religious groups in the seventeenth century.

A seventeenth century illustration of the Ranters.

TASKS...

1 Draw a line like the one below and place the different religious groups on the line as you think the government might have seen them.

Complete
approval

Complete
disapproval

EXTENSION TASK

2 Find out two things about The Society of Friends today which make it different from other Protestant groups.

Case study: The Levellers

Some of the religious groups had ideas about changing other things as well as religion. Some of them wanted to alter the way the country was run. The government thought this made them very dangerous. Cromwell thought the biggest threat came from the Levellers.

TASKS...

1 Write a list of questions you might ask in order to find out if the Levellers really were dangerous.

2 Now see if you can find the answers to your questions from the evidence in the boxes below. Write down your answers.

The evidence

Many Levellers lived in London. Some were shopkeepers and apprentices. There were a lot of Levellers in Cromwell's New Model Army. Many soldiers had not been paid by Parliament for months. They were angry that they had helped to defeat the king but were not being rewarded for their efforts.

The Levellers were led by John Lilburne. He had been in Parliament's army but quarrelled with his commanding officer. In 1649 he was put on trial for treason when he criticised Cromwell and Parliament. He was found not guilty. But he continued to criticise the government. He was sent out of the country in 1651, but after he came back to England in 1653 he was put in prison where he died in 1657.

After the king's execution, there was a lot of unrest. A Leveller soldier was shot for mutiny. His funeral in London turned into a demonstration. The mourners wore green ribbons - the Leveller colour.

Colonel Rainsborough, an important Leveller, said: 'I think that the poorest man in England has a life just like the greatest man; every man who has to live under a government should first agree to be ruled by that government.'

The Levellers put some demands to Parliament in May 1649. These included the following:

• Parliament should be chosen by men over 21 years.
• People accused of crimes should be tried by jury.
• People should be allowed to follow any religion they like.
• The death penalty should only be for murder.
• People of each **parish** should choose their own church ministers.
• No one accused of a crime should be forced to give evidence against themselves.
• All money for the government should be raised by taxing property.

The harvest of 1649 was very bad. In the winter, food prices were high and poor people went hungry. People had thought that now the king was dead their lives would get better. Now it seemed as if life was just as bad, if not worse.

Key words

Banish To stop somebody from living in their country.
Parish The area around a church.

TASKS...

1 Copy out and finish the speech bubbles below. You will need to show that you understand what each person would have said if they had been asked about their views on the Levellers. Consider all the evidence before you begin. **WS**

I'm very poor. I just manage to scrape a living and so I think ...

I'm used to having a say in how the country should be run and so I think ...

A woman who lives in a small village and who farms the land for her living.

A landowner who has a lot of money.

Now that the king has gone, I have even more power and so I think ...

I helped to put this country where it is today and so I think ...

An MP who is a Puritan.

A soldier of the New Model Army who hasn't been paid for months.

Cromwell had to decide what, if anything, should be done about the Levellers.

💡 Have you answered all your questions? What would you have decided about the Levellers?

What did happen to the Levellers?

In May 1649, 1200 Levellers tried to overthrow the government. They were cornered by Oliver Cromwell in Oxfordshire. Most ran away or gave in. The rest - about 340 - were locked up in a church for three days. Then, three were shot in front of the others. The Leveller revolt was over.

Plenary

Here are the answers! Work out the questions.

1 Baptists and The Society of Friends.

2 The Fifth Monarchists.

3 Because they hadn't been paid.

4 Trial by jury, freedom of worship and no accused person to be forced to give evidence against themselves.

WHAT DIFFERENT PROBLEMS DID JAMES I AND JAMES II FACE IN THE SEVENTEENTH CENTURY?

WAS GUY FAWKES FRAMED?

Objectives

In this section you will:
- look at different views of the Gunpowder Plot
- decide if you think Guy Fawkes was framed.

Starter

SOURCE A

A print from 1605 showing the execution of the Gunpowder plotters.

Imagine that there was television in 1605. You are a reporter at the scene shown in Source A. You have one minute to tell viewers what is happening. Write out what you would say.

The Gunpowder Plot

On 5 November 1605 James I was due in Parliament. The Lords and MPs would be in the House of Lords to hear him speak. James and his government were Protestants.

On the evening of 4 November a message was passed to Lord Monteagle, a Catholic. It advised him not to go to Parliament. He showed it to Robert Cecil, who was James's chief adviser. Cecil sent men to search the Parliament building.

In a cellar, under the House of Lords, they found 36 barrels of gunpowder and Guy Fawkes, a Catholic. He was preparing the fuse to be lit when Parliament met. Catholics believed that James, a Protestant, should not be king.

Historians agree that gunpowder was found there, and that Fawkes was going to light the fuse, and that he was arrested. But there are two theories about the Gunpowder Plot.

Theory 1
Robert Cecil only found out just in time about the plot because of the message to Lord Monteagle.

Theory 2
Robert Cecil already knew about the plot through spies, and he allowed the plotters to go ahead. He even made it easy for them to get gunpowder, so that he could catch them in the act. This would give him an excuse to **persecute** Catholics in England.

Key words

Persecute To cause people to suffer because of their beliefs.

TASKS...

1 In groups, look at the evidence shown in Sources B-H on pages 79-80.

   a) Which sources support Theory 1?

   b) Which sources support Theory 2?

   Write down your answers in your book.

SOURCE B

I care for your safety. So I would advise you to miss this Parliament. Think of some excuse. Go into the country, for they shall receive a terrible blow this Parliament – and yet they shall not see who hurts them.

From the letter delivered to Lord Monteagle on 26 October 1605.

SOURCE C

He said he intended to set fire to the fuse when the king came into the Houses of Parliament. The powder would blow up a quarter of an hour later.

From the confession of Guy Fawkes after he had been tortured.

SOURCE D

Two signatures by Guy Fawkes. The first one is his usual signature. The second one is from his confession after he was tortured.

SOURCE E

The plan was the idea of Robert Catesby, a Catholic. They would blow up the Houses of Parliament when King James I went there to make a speech.

At 7 pm on 26 October, Lord Monteagle was brought a letter. It had been given to his servant by a stranger. The letter was written by Francis Tresham, one of the plotters and Lord Monteagle's cousin. The letter warned him not to attend Parliament. Monteagle took it at once to Robert Cecil, the king's chief minister. Cecil took the letter to the king.

On 4 November, the cellar was searched. They found gunpowder and Guy Fawkes was arrested. In the Tower of London he was tortured and he confessed about the plot.

The events according to Robert Cecil.

A seventeenth-century drawing showing how Britain was saved from 'Catholic plots'. On the left is the Spanish Armada. In the centre, the Pope and his cardinals are plotting. On the right, Guy Fawkes is in the cellar – but with God watching him.

Here are more details about the Gunpowder Plot:

- Cecil's spies were always watching Catholics.
- The cellar was owned by a government official.
- At the time, the government controlled all gunpowder. All supplies were kept in the Tower of London. How did the plotters get their supplies?
- Was the letter to Monteagle a fake?

- Monteagle's name was removed from all accounts given about the plotters. He was given money by the government.
- When the plotters were arrested on 7 November, the government seemed to have known in advance where they all were.

Some people are sure that there was foul play. They think that some of the government secretly arranged to arrest the plotters.

Written by an Italian (Catholic) visitor in 1605.

An extract from a modern textbook.

TASKS...

1 Do these sources give information you can trust about the Gunpowder Plot?

a) Do a reliability check on five of the sources to decide how far you can trust them. Ask yourself:
- Who wrote or drew it?
- Would they be likely to be biased (give only one side of the story)?
- Why did they write or draw it?

b) Make a copy of the table below and give each of the five sources a rating of 1–5 (1 = totally unreliable; 5 = very reliable). Explain your decisions. An example is done for you.

Source	Rating (1–5)	Reason
J	2	He was a Catholic who would be against James and would support the plotters

2 Now that you have thought about the reliability of each source, think about the key question again:

Was Guy Fawkes framed? Use the following guide to help with your answer.

- Write an introduction that sets out the issues and states your aims.
- Put each new point in a separate paragraph. Start each paragraph with a sentence on a new topic, to introduce the new point you are going to make.
- Use evidence from your reading to support your arguments. Use words such as *for example, such as, for instance*.
- Use quotes from your reading to support your arguments.
- Use words like *equally, whereas, similarly,* to connect your points when you compare or contrast.
- Write a summary (conclusion) that sets out your overall opinion on the question.

Plenary

Here are the answers! Work out what the questions could be.

1 To blow up the king and the House of Lords.
2 The letter warned Lord Monteagle not to go to the House of Lords.
3 Catholics became even more unpopular.

WAS THE 'GLORIOUS REVOLUTION' INEVITABLE?

Objectives

In this section you will try to decide:
- why James II upset so many people
- whether he could have prevented the 'Glorious **Revolution**'.

Starter

Read Source A.

Imagine a group of Catholics attacking your wives, smashing your children's brains against the walls, or cutting your throats. Imagine seeing your mother or father being burned alive. This is what people saw the last time Catholics ruled us.

From a pamphlet printed in London in 1679.

What view does this pamphlet give of Catholics? According to Source A, would a Catholic king be popular in England?

Key words

Revolution The overthrow of a government by force.

The 'Glorious Revolution'

Read the following information about the events leading to the Glorious Revolution. Try to think of reasons why the 'Glorious Revolution' took place.

The events of 1688 have been called the 'Glorious Revolution'. The unpopular King James II was replaced by his daughter, Mary, and her husband, William of Orange. The change took place peacefully, without a civil war.

Why did the English Parliament want to replace James II? The Glorious Revolution took place because, during his brief reign, James II managed to upset many of his people.

How did James II upset so many people?

Marriage
In 1672 James II declared himself a Catholic and married his second wife, Mary of Modena, who was a Catholic.

Archbishop and bishops
From April 1687 James allowed all Christians, including Catholics, to worship as they wished. The Archbishop of Canterbury and six other bishops protested against these changes. The king had them arrested and put on trial.

In August 1688, the court found them not guilty. There were many celebrations as this was the first time that an English king had lost a court case.

Catholics
From 1687 James II allowed Catholics to worship freely. He appointed Catholics as ministers and officers in the army – all without the permission of Parliament.

The 'warming pan' baby
In June 1688 James's wife gave birth to a son. This meant that James II now had a male heir who would be Catholic. But some people did not believe it was their child. His wife had already had several miscarriages.

Rumours spread that the baby had been smuggled into the palace in a **warming pan**.

Monmouth Rebellion
In 1685 James II crushed this Protestant rebellion. About 250 people were hanged, drawn and quartered, and 1000 people were sent away to the West Indies where they were sold as slaves.

Standing army
James II used the excuse of the Monmouth Rebellion to build up a large army.

Government
James II began appointing Catholics as government ministers and sacked all ministers who opposed him.

SOURCE B

II ◇

The Queen is brought to bed of a Boy

Reported so

A playing card from 1689, showing how the baby might have been smuggled in.

TASKS...

1 Draw a mind map to show the reasons why the Glorious Revolution took place.

2 You are an adviser to James II. What advice would you give him to prevent the 'Glorious Revolution'? Write your advice in the form of a memo to the king:

Memo

To: King James II
From:
Date:
Subject:

To avoid a possible revolution I suggest that...

Plenary

Write a headline for a tabloid newspaper article, to announce that James II is no longer the king.

HOW 'GLORIOUS' WAS THE REVOLUTION?

Objectives

In this section you will try to decide:
- how peaceful was the revolution?
- how much change did it bring?

Starter

SOURCE **A**

A painting showing William and his troops landing in Devon in 1688.

SOURCE **B**

A Dutch engraving of the Revolution of 1688 with William and Mary on the right.

Sources A and B give very different views of the Glorious Revolution. What differences are there between the two sources? Can you think of one reason why they are so different?

The 'Glorious Revolution' – the events

The revolution was seen as 'Glorious' because it was peaceful, popular with almost everyone and brought about many changes.

TASKS...

1 Look at the statements about the Glorious Revolution below. Put the statements into two lists:

• One list to show that the revolution was 'Glorious'.
• One list to show that it was not. Some statements may not fit into either list! **WS**

1   Powerful people invited the Dutch prince, William of Orange, to invade England and make himself king.

2   William and Mary were Protestants and were more popular than the Catholic James II.

3   Under William and Mary, Parliament was given the power to pass laws and control the army.

4   On 4 November 1688 William landed in Devon with 15,000 soldiers. They marched towards London and were cheered on their way as 'Protestant saviours'. They were joined by supporters who pinned orange colours on their shirts.

5   In 1689 James II landed in Ireland and began to help the Irish Catholics. He took land back from the Protestant settlers.

6   In 1689 William and Mary were presented with the Bill of Rights. This said that they had to obey the laws of England and could only change them with Parliament's permission.

7   James II died in 1702.

8   In Ireland, in 1689, many Protestants fled to Londonderry to get away from James II and his troops. They surrounded the city. The *siege* lasted for 105 days. About 15,000 Protestants died.

9   William and Mary had not become king and queen because of **birthright**. Parliament had invited them to become rulers of England.

10 In December 1688 William sent his troops to London. They took over Whitehall Palace. The next day James II left and sailed down the Thames, before travelling to France.

11 William came to England because he wanted to become more powerful. He hoped to get the support of England in his war against the Catholic king of France, Louis XIV.

12 James II's first wife died in 1671. They had two daughters, Mary and Anne.

13 William and his army went to Ireland in 1690. They defeated James II's Catholic army at the Battle of the Boyne on 1 July 1690.

14 After the defeat of James II in Ireland, William was popular with Irish Protestants but not with Catholics. Over 4000 Catholics lost their land and Catholics were not allowed to be soldiers or teachers.

15 The Bill of Rights said that no Catholic could ever become king of England.

16 In 1694 **Nonconformists** were allowed to worship freely.

Key words

Siege A military blockade of a city.
Birthright Something a person is entitled to because of the family they are born into.
Nonconformist Any Protestant who was not a member of the Church of England.

TASKS...

Now look again at your two lists.

1 Do you think it was a Glorious Revolution? Explain how it was peaceful, popular, and meant that there was still a king.

2 Can you think of a better word to describe the revolution than 'Glorious'? Write this down.

Plenary

Draw a sketch to show how the powers of the king and queen changed because of the 'Glorious Revolution'.

Now compare it to someone else's in your class. What is similar or different?

THEME: RELIGION AND INTERNAL POLITICS

CONCLUSION

In this theme you have learned a lot about religion and politics. It is often difficult to separate them. Was Elizabeth I's quarrel with Philip II of Spain about religion or about politics? Were the causes of the Civil War religious - or political?

When the ruler of England was Catholic, then everyone had to be Catholic, as in Mary I's reign. When the ruler was Protestant, then the religion of the country was Protestant, for example in James I's reign.

You can get an overview of how religion and politics affected people's lives in the period 1500-1570 by making your own timeline.

Using a piece of landscape A3 paper plot on it:

- the reigns of each ruler
- examples of times when religion changed
- examples of times when there were important political events.

An example has been started for you below.

Ruler	James II, 1685-8
Main Religion	Catholic
Political Events	Monmouth Rebellion, 1685 Glorious Revolution, 1688

Leave space at the bottom to add some more rows for each ruler. You can then add information from the next two themes. You will be able to build up your timeline into an overview of the whole period.

THEME: SOCIAL LIFE

INTRODUCTION

Do you think about what class you are? In the sixteenth and seventeenth centuries the social class you were born into decided almost everything about you. Rich and poor people led separate lives. They dressed differently, did different jobs and even ate different food. What class you were made a difference between having a good life and a poor one.

Five hundred years ago people's lives were very different from ours. Ordinary people had to work very hard just to survive. Getting enough to eat was what was most important to them. Their lives were often short. When people became ill they did not know what caused it. They believed in demons, devils and that God punished them if they sinned. They believed in witches, too. Life was difficult and often dangerous. There was no police force but when criminals were caught they were punished harshly. Plotting against the king or queen, stealing, begging and witchcraft might all be punished by death. After all, death happened every day. People were used to it. They were often in pain so it was not surprising that pain was also used to punish people.

Rich people had better homes and food than the poor but they still had many of the same problems. They might live better from day to day but many of them died young. A lot of women died in childbirth.

All this doesn't mean that people lived sad and dull lives. Most people were able to have fun. They enjoyed their leisure time, even though they didn't have televisions or computers. Pleasures were simple. Their lives were well ordered and everybody knew where they stood in society. People knew what to expect from life and got on with living.

6

HOW DID PEOPLE LIVE IN THE SIXTEENTH AND SEVENTEENTH CENTURIES?

HOW WERE PEOPLE DIVIDED IN SOCIETY?

Objectives

In this section you will understand:
- how people were divided into classes
- that each of the four main classes lived very different lives.

You will be able to:
- explain how people enjoyed their leisure time.

Starter

Think about the things in your home that you couldn't live without.

💡 *Brainstorm which things you need to survive.*

💡 *Brainstorm which things are luxuries - things you don't really need.*

💡 *Compare your lists with others in your class.*

In Tudor times there were also things people needed and things they could do without. Below is a list of some of these. Sort them into two groups, those that were needed and those they could have done without.

Window glass   Wax candles   Mattresses

Cooking pots

Silk and velvet clothes   Linen clothes

Room for all the family

Room for the animals in winter   Fire for cooking

Feather bed   Woollen clothes

Toys

Separate rooms for sleeping and living

Which different classes of people were there in Tudor and Stuart times?

A churchman called William Harrison who lived in Elizabeth I's reign wrote:

We divide our people into four sorts: gentlemen,[1] citizens[2] or burgesses, yeomen[3] and labourers.[4]

He meant:

1

Lords and other rich people who owned land and had many servants.

2

Rich townspeople
– usually merchants and traders.

3

Farmers who owned or rented land.
Sometimes they had people working for them.

4

Poor farm workers who worked for landowners.

TASKS...

1 Look at the pictures of the gentleman, citizen, yeoman and labourer. Write down which of the descriptions below goes with each picture.

How could you tell who was in each class?

| **A gentleman.** | **A citizen.** | **A yeoman.** | **A labourer.** |

A He lives in a small village and doesn't often leave it, as he has to walk everywhere. He works very hard - ploughing, weeding, looking after animals and mending fences. He does what he's told to do on the lord's farm.

B He has a huge house with beautiful gardens and large farms. He spends a lot of time in London at the king or queen's court but his wife and family stay in the country.

C He has quite a good life. He owns some land and rents more. He works very hard and can afford to send his children to school.

D He lives in the town and makes quite a lot of money selling cloth. He has a big house which is also his office. He is very important in the running of the town.

At this time it was difficult to move up into a higher class, even if you made a lot of money. Your home, job and even your clothes told people what class you were.

SOURCE A

A painting of the guests at a wedding celebration near London in the sixteenth century.

Which classes of people can you see in Source A? What are they doing? (There is more than one class.)

TASKS...

1 Look at Sources B–K. Then decide which sources are about each class. Use what you have read to help you.

2 Copy the table below and write in your answers.

Class	Sources describing each class
Gentlemen	
Citizens	
Yeomen	
Labourers	

SOURCE B

My father was a yeoman. He rented a farm for £3 or £4 a year. He farmed as much land as six men. He kept 100 sheep and my mother milked 30 cows. He sent me to school. He gave money to poor neighbours.

Bishop Hugh Latimer speaking in the early sixteenth century.

SOURCE C

This house was built in Suffolk in the late sixteenth century.

SOURCE D

The inside of a house built at the end of the sixteenth century.

The Earl of Arundel came in, dressed in gold and patterned armour, with 22 gentlemen. They wore red velvet, yellow satin jackets and red velvet boots.

Description of a tournament in 1651.

Key words

Tournament A sporting event for knights.
Burgess A type of citizen.

A drawing of a home built in the eighteenth century.

Citizens and **burgesses** are rich enough to be in charge of running towns.

William Harrison writing in the late sixteenth century.

Working in the fields, shown in a seventeenth century painting.

HOW DID PEOPLE LIVE?

95

The fourth and last sort of people are poor farmworkers.

William Harrison.

SOURCE

The bedroom of a house built during the seventeenth century.

A home built during the late sixteenth century.

TASKS...

Work in a group.

1 Choose one class of people. Make a list of:
   a) all the good things about being this class
   b) all the bad things about being this class.

2 Create a profile for a member of this group.

You should include their:
- name, date of birth and address
- education and training
- jobs held/experience
- manners and behaviour.

If you have time, you could illustrate your work.

Plenary

These are the answers! Now what are the questions?

- They went to fairs twice a year.
- They wore silk and velvet clothes.
- At court.
- Citizens.

HOW DID PEOPLE ENJOY THEIR LEISURE TIME?

Objectives

By the end of this section you will know:
- what fun and sports rich and poor people enjoyed
- if a person's class affected the sports they liked.

You will be able to:
- use sources to find out how rich and poor people enjoyed themselves.

Starter

How many games can you see in Source A? What are they?

Which of these games are still played today?

SOURCE A

A painting showing different games which were popular in the sixteenth century.

What sports and entertainments were there and who enjoyed them?

TASKS...

1 As you study the information in this section, list the sports and entertainments. Divide them into:
- sports people do
- sports people watch.

2 Try to decide which would have been for the rich and which for the poor. Are there any which would have been for both?

Everyone tries to throw his opponent on his nose, even on hard stone. Sometimes their necks are broken, sometimes their legs, sometimes their arms and sometimes their noses bleed badly. Everyone is hurt.

Football was played in towns and villages. The idea was to get the ball into your own parish. It was very violent, as this spectator noted.

In the countryside all classes enjoyed hunting. Rich people rode and poor people walked behind the hunt. Sometimes poor people killed rabbits on their lord's land. Laws were passed to try to stop people from **poaching**.

At Christmas time, the lord organised food and drink and fun for his rich friends and the poor people of the village. There was eating, dancing, games and singing.

An extract from a modern history book on Tudor England.

Key words

Poaching Killing and stealing animals (for example, pheasants, deer or rabbits) from a rich person's land.

Plays became very popular in Queen Elizabeth's reign. Theatres were built, like the Globe and the Rose in London. People of all classes began going to them. William Shakespeare, Christopher Marlowe and many other famous writers had their plays performed in Elizabeth I's time.

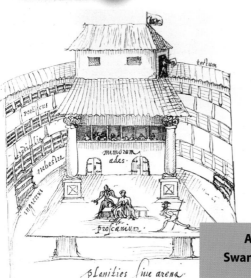

A drawing of the old Swan Theatre in the late sixteenth century.

21 December 1663:
Went to Shoe Lane to see a cock-fight. Saw some strange people, from Members of Parliament to the poorest people, bakers and butchers and so on. And all of them swearing and betting.

From *The Diary of Samuel Pepys*.

The last chance for fun before Lent was known as Shrovetide (we still have pancakes on Shrove Tuesday). It was a dull and difficult time of the year. Food supplies were running low. It was then that 'threshing the cock' took place (Source F).

All classes of people enjoyed dancing. Dancing was important as it was the main way in which men and women met each other.

Key words

Flail An instrument used for beating things, with a wooden handle at the end and a shorter stick that swings freely.

A cock was tied up and people tried to kill it by throwing things at it. If you killed the cock you won it. Sometimes the cock would be buried with its head sticking out of the ground and blindfolded people would try to kill it with a **flail**.

An account from the time of 'threshing the cock'.

SOURCE G

Dancing is done to see if lovers are fit and healthy. They are allowed to kiss each other so they can tell if they give off a bad smell.

From a book on dancing by a Frenchman.

SOURCE H

A painting showing Elizabeth I dancing at court with Robert Dudley, Earl of Leicester.

Fairs were a lot of fun for everybody. There were jugglers, acrobats, fire-eaters, musicians and all sorts of actors. There was lots of food drink, games and gambling.

A large bear was tied up. Then some big dogs were brought in to attack the bear. The bear's teeth were blunted so they could not injure the dogs. People only helped the bear when the dogs had almost killed it.

Written by a German visitor to London, in 1599. Elizabeth I used to enjoy entertainments such as bear-baiting.

Key words

Bait Allowing dogs to attack a chained animal.

SOURCE J

A drawing of a fair in the seventeenth century.

TASKS...

1 Imagine that you are a poor young man in the time of Elizabeth I. You are able to swap lives with a rich young lord for a week and enjoy his social life. Send a postcard home. In it describe the fun you have.

Plenary

What do you think would have been your favourite way of enjoying yourself at this time? What would you not have liked?

HOW HARD WAS LIFE FOR WOMEN?

Objectives

By the end of this section you will know:
- why lots of women lived hard and difficult lives
- why rich women didn't always have better lives than poor women.

You will be able to:
- assess evidence about women's lives.

Starter

You now know a lot about life in the sixteenth and seventeenth centuries. Think about where today's women would stand on this line.

●━━━━━━━━━━━━━━━━━━━━━━━━━━━━━━━━●

Women lived poor and
miserable lives.

Women lived satisfying and
happy lives.

💡 *Where do you think women at the time would have put themselves? When you have learned more about women's lives, you will be asked to do this again. This time you will need evidence to back up your decision.*

What was the place of women in society?

The information on pages 102–9 and Sources A-R look at:

- what people thought about women

- women's rights

- how women spent their time

- the problems women faced.

They will give you a better picture of the difficulties women faced in the sixteenth and seventeenth centuries.

TASKS...

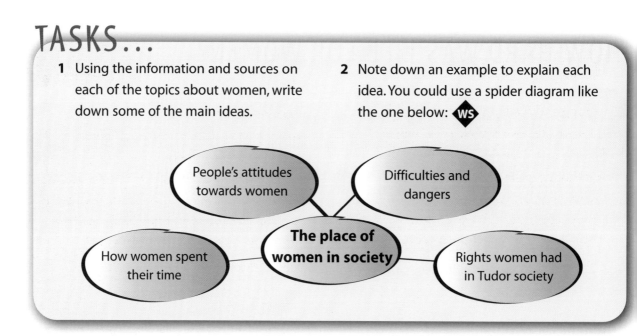

1 Using the information and sources on each of the topics about women, write down some of the main ideas.

2 Note down an example to explain each idea. You could use a spider diagram like the one below: **WS**

- People's attitudes towards women
- Difficulties and dangers
- How women spent their time
- **The place of women in society**
- Rights women had in Tudor society

What were people's attitudes toward women?

SOURCE A

In a Tudor home the wife was in charge of running the house. But if her husband didn't like something she did, he would punish her. By law, a man could beat his wife, but his stick was not supposed to be thicker than his thumb.

A modern historian.

SOURCE B

A cartoon from the sixteenth century showing a husband beating his wife.

SOURCE C

Educating women and taming foxes has the same effect. It makes them more cunning.

King James I.

SOURCE D

The husband has authority over everyone else in the family. He is a king in his own house.

From a book written in 1622.

28 February 1665:

I checked my wife's kitchen accounts at the end of the month and found 7 shillings missing. I called her 'beggar' and she told me off ... I find she is very sneaky. She is always plotting in her mind ... We argued and I went to my office.

From *The Diary of Samuel Pepys*.

19 December 1664:

I was very angry and told my wife off for not giving her servants orders properly. She gave me a cross answer, and I hit her over her left eye. She was in great pain, but she tried to bite and scratch me ... I was very upset to think what I had done. She had to put a **poultice** on her eye, and it turned black.

From *The Diary of Samuel Pepys*.

Key words

Poultice A bandage containing ointment to help injuries heal.

It wasn't just men who kept women in their place. Other women did too!

Too many women now behaved like men ... the war had allowed them to walk about with a snooty attitude, to gamble, to drink, to party and to quarrel.

The Duchess of Newcastle complaining about the behaviour of women after the Civil War.

What rights did women have in Tudor and Stuart society?

In 1500, women did not have many rights. When a woman got married everything she owned became her husband's - even their children.

Marriage

Many girls' parents would pick husbands for them. When a woman got married she had to bring her husband a present called a **dowry**. This could be a few sheep or it might be land, money and jewels. Girls from rich families were often married very young. Their parents wanted to be friends with another family and this was a way of doing it. They went to live with their husbands when they were older.

How did women spend their time?

How women spent their time depended on their position in society.

The rich

A rich lady did not have to do housework or look after her children. She had servants for those things. Instead, she checked up on her servants. She read books and did sewing. Everything had to be ready for when her husband came home from court or his business.

A painting of a wealthy lady.

SOURCE I

They spend time walking, riding, playing cards and visiting friends. England is called the paradise of married women.

A Dutch man's description of women's life in England in 1575.

A merchant's wife would help her husband to run his business as well as looking after the house. She worked hard but she had a nice home, servants, fine clothes and good food.

The poor

In the country a poor woman helped her husband in the fields, cooked, looked after the children, spun wool and mended clothes. It was a hard life. If he was quite well off then she would have servants to help her. If he was a labourer working for the local landowner, then she would have to do everything herself. She would also help her husband in the fields at busy times such as harvest.

SOURCE J

Key words

Winnow To shake out corn to separate the grain from the chaff (the bits of husk surrounding the grain).

It is a wife's job to **winnow** corn, to make malt, to make hay and cut corn. She should help her husband fill the muck waggon, drive the plough, load hay, go to market to sell butter, cheese, milk, eggs, chickens, pigs, geese and corn.

From Anthony Fitzherbert's, *Book of Husbandry*, written in 1523.

What difficulties and dangers did women face in their everyday lives?

Many people died of diseases because no one knew much about them or how to cure them. Marriages didn't last long because one of the partners would die.

Childbirth

One in three babies died before they were a year old. Childbirth was also very dangerous for women. People did not know how to deal with the problems which often happened in childbirth. They didn't keep things clean because they did not know this was important. Even rich people and queens died giving birth.

SOURCE K

A sixteenth century engraving. Giving birth at this time was dangerous.

SOURCE L

Mistress Earnshaw of York had a painful **labour**, and her child was pulled from her slowly. She died, leaving a sad husband.

This death in childbirth was recorded in 1684.

Pregnancy

Women who had babies when they were not married were seen as wicked. Some tried to hide their pregnancy because their parents would throw them out and they might starve. They sometimes dumped or killed their child. They could be hanged for this. It was different for a man. There was no shame and he didn't have to support the mother or baby. There was no way of proving the child was his.

SOURCE M

Do not tell me any more about your love for me. My marriage is up to my parents. If I do not do as they wish they will no longer support me.

Written by a young lady to Thomas Wythorne, a court musician, 1558. She did not marry him, but later married a richer man of her parents' choosing.

SOURCE N

16-year-old Lady Jane Grey was beaten by her father until she agreed to marry Lord Guilford Dudley. This was part of a plot to make Jane queen when Edward VI died.

A modern historian.

What control did women have over their own lives?

Women and marriage

💡 Why did women get married? Surely it would have been better for them to stay single?

If a woman did not have a husband, brother or father she would find it difficult to support herself. Even if she owned a house and land, men would probably not take her seriously. She might be cheated by her servants. Her lands and property might be stolen. She might even be forced to marry. Most women married the man their parents chose for them. However, some women were determined to marry for love so they stood up to their parents.

Women needed men to support them. A woman on her own had to live with relatives. They often made her life miserable. After Henry VIII closed the monasteries and convents, single women couldn't even become nuns.

Single women in the country found life very hard. They couldn't plough the fields and cut the crops on their own. They tried to earn money by spinning wool. Many 'spinster' aunts lived with their families.

SOURCE O

The women of England are pretty. They have a lot of freedom and make good use of it. They often walk around or drive in a coach in beautiful clothes. Men have to put up with such behaviour and can't punish them for it.

From Thomas Platter, *Travels in England*, 1599.

SOURCE P

A portrait of Bess of Hardwick (1520-1608).

Could women ever be independent and successful?

Bess of Hardwick was a gentleman's daughter in the sixteenth century. She was clever and good looking and had three husbands. They all left her lands and money when they died. When she fell out with her fourth husband, she took him to court to get property and money. She was one of the most powerful and wealthy women in England and became famous for building grand houses.

Bess was an unusual woman in the sixteenth century. But many women of different classes made successful and happy lives for themselves.

The wives of merchants helped their husbands to run their businesses. If their husband died, they might be able to keep the business going which meant they could still live well.

SOURCE Q

Alice Chester of Bristol continued her husband's trade, importing iron from Spain. She did so well that she gave the city a crane for the docks and a fine carved wooden screen for one of the city's churches.

From a modern history textbook.

Women during wartime

In times of crisis, men often had to rely on their wives. During the Civil War (1642-9) many women were left in charge of their homes when their husbands went to fight. Sometimes they were attacked by the enemy and had to use their intelligence to beat them. Some even acted like army commanders. They gave orders to the servants on how to fight and bargained with the enemy when they had to give in.

Some women saw the Civil War as a chance to be different. Some became spies, others followed their husbands to war. Others even pretended to be men and fought in battles (see Source R).

An engraving showing a woman who disguised herself as a drummer boy in the Civil War. She was only discovered when she gave birth.

TASKS...

1 Look back at the information and the sources. Make three sets of bullet points to show ways in which women's live were dangerous, ways in which they worked hard and ways in which they enjoyed themselves. They might look like this:

How women's lives were dangerous
- *having a baby outside marriage*
-
-

How women worked hard
- *working in the fields*
-
-

How women enjoyed themselves
- *visiting friends*
-
-

Plenary

○━━━━━━━━━━━━━━━━━━━━━━━━━━━━━━━━━○

Women lived poor and miserable lives.

Women lived satisfying and happy lives.

Remember where you placed Tudor and Stuart women on the line? Has your opinion changed now? If so, list three things which have changed your mind. If not, list three things to back up your opinion.

DID PEOPLE EAT A HEALTHY DIET?

Objectives

By the end of this section, you will understand:
- why the rich and poor had very different diets
- how healthy the diets of the rich and poor were.

You will be able to:
- balance and combine sets of evidence.

Starter

All of the foods below are eaten by people somewhere in the world. A lot of them are eaten in Britain. For example, black pudding is made of pig's blood. Sheep's stomach is used to make haggis.

	cabbage	dog		dandelion leaves
		horse	nettles	
peacock	oysters			veal
peas	swan		cactus	
pig's blood		lamb		snails
	rabbit	sheep's stomach		

Which of these foods would you eat? Which ones would you not eat? Why?

Which foods did people eat?

What we eat today depends on:
- how we have been brought up
- the country we live in
- what food is available
- what we can afford.

Many of the foods we eat today were not around in Britain in the sixteenth and seventeenth centuries. It took a long time to bring goods from other countries. Some countries had not yet been discovered. There were no fridges to keep foods fresh.

TASKS...

1 In a group, work out which of these foods people would not have had in 1500. Give reasons. (Clue: Think about where they come from and how easy it was to transport them.)

apples	*oysters*	*runner beans*
cabbage	*peacock*	*spinach*
chocolate	*pickled herrings*	*tea*
coffee	*pigeon*	*tomatoes*
hare	*pineapple*	*turkey*
kangaroo	*potatoes*	*venison*
lemons	*rice*	

Daily bread and beer

Everyone ate a lot of bread. In large houses it was baked every day. Poor people needed bread to stay alive. When times were really hard, bread was sometimes made from beans or peas or even acorns.

People drank a lot of weak beer. It was safer to drink than water, which was often dirty.

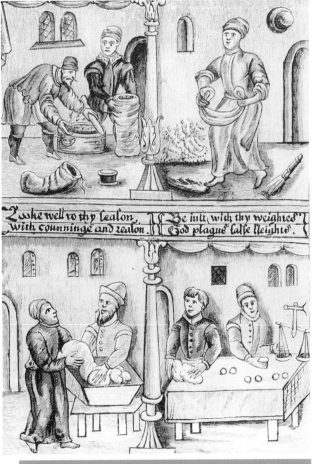

An illustration from the 1598 *Ordinances of the York Bakers' Company*.

Key words

Pickled herrings Fish preserved in salt water and vinegar.
Venison Deer.

HOW DID PEOPLE LIVE?

111

Storing food

Food was kept in barrels because there were no fridges. There was no food for the animals in the winter so most were killed in the autumn. Meat was salted so that it would last for months. Rich people also salted and bottled vegetables and made jam out of fruit. Poor people could not afford to do this.

TASKS...

1 Look at the statements below. They are about what people ate and the effects their diet might have had on them.

Match up the causes with the consequences. One has been done for you. **WS**

CAUSES

I	When harvests failed poor people went hungry.
2	Rich people ate three meals a day. Often they had seven courses.
3	Most animals were killed in the autumn. This meant that in the spring there was no meat to eat.
4	Rich people ate sweets and cakes between meals.
5	Most poor people ate bread made from rye or barley.
6	Rich people ate lots of meat and fat.

CONSEQUENCES

A	Whole grain bread is good for you.
B	Over-eating can cause heart attacks.
C	Too much sugar rots teeth.
D	Too much meat and fat makes people ill.
E	Hungry people become ill easily.
F	Lack of protein (which comes from meat), can make people ill.

How healthy were the meals of the rich and the poor?

💡 Have you had a special meal recently - for a birthday, or a wedding? What did you eat? Read Sources B–D. Which would you like best - your meal or a feast in Tudor or Stuart times?

SOURCE B

Venison, lamb, pork, veal

Roast goose, duck, pheasant

Fruit pies, jellies of all colours in the shape of birds

Quince marmalade

Marzipan, sugarbread, gingerbread

In Elizabeth I's reign, a rich merchant served this meal to special guests.

SOURCE C

Every day there were 20 dishes of food at each course and there were three courses. My host drank lots of wine. He drank two bottles at one go of either a malt drink or wine and water. His doctor said that it would cure the **stones** he had in his bladder.

Sir Edward Southcote, describing the food and drink at a large country house in 1660.

Key words

Quince A golden, pear-shaped fruit.
Stones Bladder stones, a very painful condition.

SOURCE D

Breakfast:	Bread and ale
Mid-morning:	Bread, cheese and ale
Evening:	Thin soup made of water and 'pot-herbs' (for example beans, peas, onions, nettles and other wild plants and herbs). In the autumn and winter there might be some meat.

A poor person's diet in the sixteenth century.

TASKS...

1 Do you think rich people or poor people would have been healthier? There are arguments on both sides. Which do you think are the best? Fill in the following table to say what was healthy and unhealthy about each diet. **WS**

Peasant	Rich person
I think I'm healthy because: • •	I think I'm healthy because: • •
I think the rich are unhealthy because: • •	I think the poor are unhealthy because: • •

2 Which diet would you prefer to have:
   a) a rich person's from the sixteenth century, or the special meal you described earlier?
   b) a poor person's from the sixteenth century, or the food you ate yesterday?
   Give your reasons for each one. Discuss your ideas with someone else in your class.

3 In Tudor and Stuart times what people ate changed a lot from month to month. Why do you think this was? Make a list of reasons.

Plenary

What foods do you think a rich person would have put on their shopping list? Explain your choices to someone else in your class.

7

DID ELIZABETH I EFFECTIVELY TACKLE THE PROBLEM OF BEGGING?

WHY WERE PEOPLE POOR IN TUDOR TIMES?

Objectives

By the end of this section you will know:
- why people were poor in Tudor England
- why poverty increased in the sixteenth century.

You will be able to:
- present information in different ways.

Starter

Key words

Jags dirty, ragged clothes.

> Hark, hark! The dogs do bark
>
> The beggars are coming to town.
>
> Some in rags and some in **jags**
>
> And one in a velvet gown.

This Tudor nursery rhyme gives the impression that beggars travelled round in groups from town to town and that not all of them were poor. Certainly Elizabeth I's government thought that beggars were a problem and laws were passed to deal with them.

Have you seen anyone begging? Discuss with your neighbour what you feel about beggars and why you think they beg.

Do you think the reasons for begging have always been the same, or are there different reasons today?

Why were so many people poor in Tudor times?

By the end of Elizabeth I's reign there were a lot of beggars. Some rich people said this was because poor people were lazy - they would do anything to avoid work, even risk being hanged. Was this really true?

In Tudor times poor people got no help from the government. When Elizabeth I was queen (1558-1603) the government was worried about the problem of beggars. There were more and more poor people without jobs and they were beginning to cause difficulties.

Elizabeth I's government was worried because gangs of beggars, or **vagrants**, were moving from town to town. They were tricking people out of their money. There was no police force like we have today and so it was quite difficult to stop this from happening.

Key words

Vagrant a tramp.
Black Death An outbreak of plague in the fourteenth century which killed millions of people across Europe.

Changes in farming

In the late Middle Ages half the people in England died from the **Black Death**. Landowners could not get enough people to work the land for them so they began to rear more sheep. One shepherd could look after a flock of sheep on his own but a lot of people were needed to harvest a field of wheat. So landowners started to enclose more land with fences and hedges to hold their new animals. These enclosures meant that poor people could not use common land for their own animals. Even though the population had started growing again by Tudor times, the number of jobs on the land had not.

SOURCE A

John Spencer (a rich landowner) changed lands to grass for sheep and other animals. Four people who had been living and working there were made unemployed by this. They were forced to become beggars.

An extract from a government report of 1517.

SOURCE B

Sheep eat up crops. Men themselves – noblemen and some abbots – leave no land for crops because they turn it all into pastures for sheep. The workers are thrown out and have no choice and must steal or beg.

Thomas More's view of the effects of enclosure in 1516.

SOURCE C

An engraving of a shepherd tending his flock in the late sixteenth century.

The cloth trade

Because more sheep were being reared, landowners and merchants were becoming rich from the cloth trade. Most villagers hoped to make a little money during the year by spinning or weaving wool. But there were bad times as well as good times.

Rising prices

During Elizabeth I's reign there were more people than jobs, so wages did not to go up. This became a big problem because food prices were going up. This was worse when there were poor harvests - and there were quite a few in the sixteenth century.

The loss of the monasteries

For hundreds of years the Church had helped poor people. Young men could get jobs as priests or monks. Single women could become nuns. Monasteries also looked after sick people and taught boys to read and write so they could get jobs. The Church also gave money to very poor people. After Henry VIII closed down the monasteries (see pages 16-20) this support for the poor and unemployed was lost.

Where could the poor get help now?

Poor people might be forced to go into a poorhouse. They would be given food and work until they found a job. But poorhouses were not very nice and, anyway, there weren't enough poorhouses to support all the poor and unemployed.

Old people often became ill and couldn't work. If a woman's husband died, she would have to care for her children alone. This could mean that the whole family was very poor.

SOURCE D

Anne Buckle is 46 and a widow. She has two children who make lace. They are very poor.

From a report made in Norwich in 1570.

TASKS...

1. Colour the boxes in your spider diagram. Use a different colour for each of the following reasons why people might have been poor:
   - *because they were lower class and couldn't get good jobs*
   - *because of landowners*
   - *because of the Church*

   Are there any boxes you haven't coloured? How do they make people poor? Remember to include a key on your diagram.

   You could also draw pictures to illustrate your spider diagram.

2. *'Poor people should go and get a job. They should stop begging.'*

   Imagine this was written by a rich man in Elizabethan times. Write a letter to reply to him. Here is a frame to start you off:

   There are lots of reasons I can't get a job. One is...

   Another reason is...

   Begging is my only choice. This is because...

   You should change your mind about beggars. You could help them instead by...

Plenary

Write two newspaper headlines telling people that the number of poor people has gone up a lot. One headline should sound as if it thinks these people are lazy. The other should sound as if it is sorry for them.

HOW DID THE DIFFERENT TYPES OF BEGGAR MAKE THEIR LIVING?

Objectives

By the end of this section you will know:
- what different types of beggar there were
- what beggars' cant was.

You will be able to:
- use beggars' cant to tell a story
- explain what beggars thought of themselves and about other people.

SOURCE (A)

A bpright Nicolas | man Wlmt. | The counterfet Nicolas | Cranke Genynges

A seventeenth-century woodcut showing Nicholas Jennings in disguise as a cripple and as a gang leader.

Key words

Counterfeit Pretend, false.
Crank In Elizabethan times this meant a sick person.

Starter

💡 *How do you think this beggar is trying to get money out of his victims?*

Nicholas Jennings was known as a **'Counterfeit Crank'**. *He would pretend to be ill so people would feel sorry for him and give him money. He would use soap to make himself foam at the mouth.*

Why was begging such a problem during Elizabeth I's reign?

Brainstorm the answer to these questions:

- 💡 How do you know what is in fashion today?
- 💡 How do you know what is going on in the world?
- 💡 How would you find out if it's going to be sunny tomorrow, or about a horrible murder ten miles away?

You have probably listed a lot of ways of getting information that Tudor and Stuart people did not have. Most people were born, grew up, lived their lives and died in the same town or village. They found out about important events, and gossip, from going to church, talking to travellers and from their rare trips to market. This meant that people did not always know about the tricks that might be played on them by con-men and beggars.

Turning to a life of crime

As you learned on pages 115-9, people became poorer in Elizabeth's reign. Some people turned to begging or a life of crime in order to make a living. Beggars stole and tried to trick people into giving them money. There were different types of beggar like the Counterfeit Crank in Source A. They each had their own nicknames. As you read about them, think about:

- 💡 Which would be best at getting money? Why?
- 💡 Which would be the most dangerous to meet?

A variety of con-men and beggars

The Abraham Man
He wore a sheet for clothing, with bare arms and legs. He would make strange noises, shout and stare in order to look mad.

The Courtesy Man
He wore smart clothes and spoke well. He persuaded people to lend him money. He then disappeared without paying it back.

The Clapper Dudgeon
He put salt on his body to make it sore, then stuck cloth onto the sores to pull the flesh away. Then he would cover his body with dirty, bloody cloths. The Clapper Dudgeon travelled round, often making five shillings a week (a good sum in those days).

The Freshwater Mariner and Counterfeit Soldier or Ruffler
The Freshwater Mariner pretended to be disabled, and said he had been wounded in a sea battle. The Counterfeit Soldier would say he was a wounded war hero. He begged for food and money or threatened people with his sword if they did not hand over their money.

The Rogue
He crawled along with a stick. He wore very old clothes and pretended to be weak and poor.

The Upright Man
He was the 'king of vagrants' and didn't beg. He just threatened people to get money. He even robbed other vagrants and also took their women.

Some women begged, too:

The Doxy

She carried all her stolen goods in a pack on her back, knitting as she walked. She fed chickens with bread on a hook and a thread. The chicken ate the bread, choked and then she hid it under her cloak.

The Dummerer

She upset people by pretending her tongue had been cut out. She made her mouth bleed and moaned. People saw the blood and gave her money.

The Bawdy Basket

She carried a basket, full of lace, pins and silk to sell. She stole clothes when they were laid out to dry and talked servants into giving her food for small worthless pieces of jewellery.

Beggars' cant

These beggars had their own slang to talk to each other so that ordinary people did not understand what they were saying. People have always used slang to their friends – people 'in the know' - who belong to their group. Today you probably use rap and street language with your friends. Beggars' cant was very much like this, as you can see from the chart below.

Beggars' cant	Meaning
maunding	begging
pannum	bread
stow you!	shut up!
peck	food
bring a waste!	get out of here!
cove	person, chap
boozing ken	pub
filch	stick
cloy	steal
mort	woman
duds	clothes
queer ken	prison
glaziers	eyes
darkmans	night
tip	give

TASKS...

1 In groups, write a play in which some beggars try to get money out of someone. When they talk to each other they will use beggars' cant. When they talk to non-beggars they will use normal English. Try to show their tricks and how successful they are.

Be ready to perform your play.

Plenary

Look at the plays written by other groups. Try to work out the beggars' cant and explain what the beggars were saying to each other.

WHY WERE THE LAWS ON BEGGING NOT WORKING?

Objectives

By the end of this section you will understand:
- what laws were passed to deal with beggars
- why the laws didn't work
- the different views on how good the Poor Law was.

You will be able to:
- explain why the laws did not stop begging
- explain how the Poor Law worked.

Starter

'To stop begging, beggars should have been hanged for a first offence.'

'Beggars weren't to blame for their situation. The government should have given them money and homes.'

If these two extreme views appeared at each end of a line across the classroom, where would you stand on the line?

💡 *How would you explain your decision?*

In groups, discuss where people chose to stand.

💡 *Do a lot of people have the same ideas? Why do you think this is?*

Why did something need to be done about begging?

There were a lot of worries for the government in Elizabeth I's reign. Spain attacked England and several people tried to kill the queen. The government did not want a lot of beggars wandering round the country stealing from people and cheating them.

The problems with beggars

- *There were a lot of beggars.*
- *A large number of beggars were criminals.*
- *Some people were really poor and could not get jobs.*
- *Beggars were difficult to catch.*

💡 Look at the problems. What might the government have done about each one? Discuss your ideas with a partner and make a list.

Who was responsible for the poor in Tudor times?

During Elizabeth's reign, each **parish** was supposed to look after its own poor people. The parish was like your local council. The man in charge of the parish was called the Justice of the Peace (JP). He had to do a lot of jobs, including looking after the poor. He was not paid and neither was his chief assistant, the Constable, whose job was to catch criminals like beggars and thieves.

Key words

Parish The area around a church.

Everybody belonged to a parish. When you were born, your name would be written in a big book called the Parish Record Book. The JP collected money from the rich people in the parish to take care of the poor. But there were more and more poor people (see pages 116-9).

💡 Why was it difficult to decide what to do about the poor in Tudor times?

What were the laws about begging and why weren't they working?

Begging was a crime. Richer people did not feel very sorry for the poor. A number of laws had been passed about begging:

LAWS ABOUT BEGGING

1531 Vagrants should be tied to a cart and whipped through the streets. They should then be sent back to their home parish.

1547 Anyone without a job for three days is a vagrant. He should be **branded** with a 'V' and made a slave of the person who reported him as being a vagrant. If he doesn't do everything his master asks, he can be whipped, put in prison or killed.

1572 Vagrants should be whipped and have a hole drilled through their ear. For a third offence they should be killed.

Key words

Branded Burnt with a hot iron. Thieves were branded with the letter 'T' on their forehead.

TASKS...

1 From what you have learnt so far about life in Elizabethan England, can you think of three reasons why the laws didn't stop begging? List these and share them with a partner.

TASKS...

2 The statements below might have happened as a result of some of the laws about begging. See if you can decide which laws might have caused these things to happen. The laws are jumbled up.

Results

A man couldn't get a job if he was branded.

JPs let beggars go free. They didn't want to hang a man just for begging.

Beggars often left their home parish because there was no work.

Laws

Vagrants could be whipped and sent back to their home parish.

Vagrants could be branded with a 'V'.

For a third offence a beggar could be executed.

3 ●━━━━━━━━━━━━━━━━━━━━━━━●

'To stop begging, beggars should have been hanged for a first offence.'

'Beggars weren't to blame for their situation. The government should have given them money and homes.'

Where would you now want to put yourself on this line? Have you changed your mind after reading this section? You should explain your decision by using what you have now learned about begging in Elizabethan England.

What did Elizabeth I's government do about the problem of begging?

Elizabeth's government passed more laws, in 1598 and 1601. These Poor Laws said that there were two different types of poor people:

The Deserving Poor	The Idle Poor
People who couldn't help being poor, for example widows with young children or the disabled.	People who were fit and healthy but too lazy to work.

The two types of poor people were to be treated very differently. The deserving poor were not seen as a threat.

The Deserving Poor
- *Each parish is to choose two 'overseers of the poor'. They will collect money from the rich to help the deserving poor. This money is called the poor rate.*
- *Only people on the Parish Register can receive help.*
- *Each parish must have a poorhouse for the poor and sick. There, they will receive help called 'indoor relief'. The poor will also do work in the poorhouse, to help pay for the system.*
- *If there is no poorhouse, the poor will be helped in their own homes. This is to be known as 'outdoor relief'.*
- **Pauper** *children will be sent to learn a trade (such as carpentry) as soon as they are old enough.*

The Idle Poor
- *Vagrants are to be whipped and sent back to the parish where they were born.*
- *Vagrants who are fit and healthy are to be made to work.*
- *If vagrants continue to beg they will be put in a House of Correction (like a prison) or hanged.*

Key words

Pauper A poor orphan.

A seventeenth-century illustration of a beggar being whipped through the streets.

The Poor Law lasted for two hundred years. It was a great success.

From a modern history textbook.

The government hoped that harsh punishment would frighten people into obeying the law. But there was still a lot of crime as people did not think they would be caught.

From a history textbook, published in 2000.

This was the first time that there was proper help for the poor. The system lasted until the nineteenth century. It was not perfect and poverty did not disappear, but it was a start.

From a modern history textbook.

TASKS...

1 What do you think the people below would have thought about the Poor Law? Write down three things that each might have said.

- Anne Jenkins, a crippled widow with four children
- Sir Henry Marston, a JP
- Amy Thatcher, who has made her living as a doxy.

Use the table on page 131 to help you write down your answers for each person.

Anne Jenkins	Sir Henry Marston	Amy Thatcher
I like the new laws because: • • •	I hope the new laws work, but they may cause me problems because: • • •	I don't like the new laws because: • • •

TASKS...

2 a) Read Source B. Does it suggest the Poor Law worked?

   b) Read Source C. Does it suggest the Poor Law worked?

   c) What is your own opinion about the Poor Law? Why?

Plenary

Look at these groups of words. For each group, choose one that is the odd one out. Be prepared to justify your choices!

Group A	1 deserving poor	2 idle poor	3 paupers
Group B	1 poorhouse	2 indoor relief	3 outdoor relief
Group C	1 unemployment	2 vagrancy	3 illness

Now try to create your own group of words with an odd one out. Try your groups on a partner.

8

DID CRIME PAY IN THE SIXTEENTH AND SEVENTEENTH CENTURIES?

HOW WAS CRIME DEALT WITH?

Objectives

By the end of this section you will know:
• why torture was used by the government in the sixteenth century.

Starter

Make a list of crimes and punishments that are common in Britain today.

Discuss the following questions in a group and share your ideas:

- *What are the worst crimes?*
- *What are the worst punishments?*
- *What is punishment for?*

Why was torture used in the sixteenth century?

Five hundred years ago life was harder:
- more children died than survived
- women died in childbirth
- wounds went bad, causing blood poisoning and death
- a lot of diseases killed people.

Punishments were also harsher than they are today:
- thieves were hanged
- queens were beheaded for adultery
- heretics were burned at the stake.

People accepted the idea of pain and suffering, so it was not surprising that pain was used on prisoners. Only the king or queen could order torture to be used, but there was more torture used in the Tudor period than at any other time.

💡 Why do you think that people in the sixteenth century thought that it was all right to use torture?

An illustration of the execution of Edmund Campion, who came to England to try to make people Catholic. He was hanged, drawn and quartered in 1581.

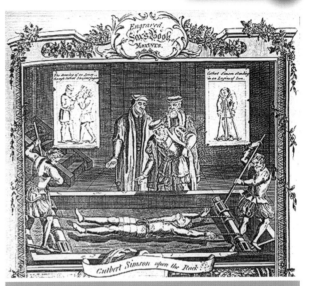

Cuthbert Simson being tortured on the rack. Simson was a Protestant. He was tortured in Queen Mary's reign, when she was trying to make England Catholic again.

His nails on all his fingers were torn and under every nail two needles were thrust in.

King James I believed in witchcraft. He accused a man called Dr Fain of causing a storm to try to wreck his ship on a sea voyage. This was one method used to get Dr Fain to confess.

In 1605 a group of Catholics planned to blow up King James I and Parliament. The first of the gang to be caught, Guy Fawkes, was questioned by the king and then tortured for information.

An extract from a modern history textbook.

TASKS...

1 Write a paragraph to answer the question:
Why was torture used in the sixteenth century? **WS**

2 Why might torture not always get the truth from the victim?

How were criminals punished?

Some prisoners were sentenced to very painful deaths. Today we would probably see these punishments as torture.

A quick way to die was by having your head chopped off, but this was only for nobles. The way traitors were killed was by hanging, drawing and quartering. The condemned men would be hanged until nearly suffocated, but were cut down before they died. Next they would be castrated (have their testicles cut off), disembowelled (have their insides torn out) and then their bowels were burnt before their eyes. Finally they were cut into four pieces which were then fixed on poles around the city.

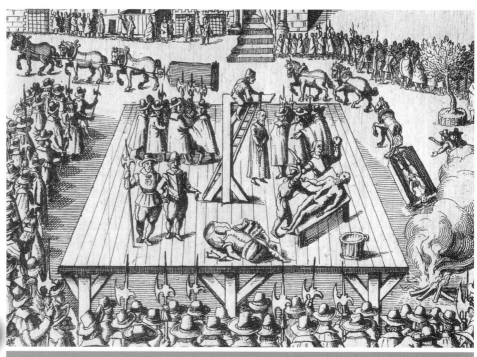

The execution of four traitors by hanging, drawing and quartering, from a print published at the time.

SOURCE F

The execution of traitors took place in public. The traitor or his family usually paid money to the executioner. They wanted him to let the traitor hang until he was dead. Or perhaps he would kill him quickly with a knife as soon as he was cut down and before his bowels were cut out. If the executioner was not paid enough, or wanted the victim to suffer, he might deliberately make the execution last longer.

An account of Tudor punishment from a modern history textbook.

SOURCE G

Noblemen were the only prisoners who were allowed to be beheaded. They usually gave the executioner a small gift, to encourage him to do his job well and quickly. Sometimes the victim died at the first stroke of the axe, but sometimes two or three chops were needed.

Another common punishment was whipping. Criminals were sometimes sentenced to be whipped through the streets tied behind a slow-moving cart. They might also be put in the stocks. They were surrounded by crowds who threw eggs, stones and rotting meat at them.

Criminals were also mutilated. This might mean having an ear nailed to the pillory or cut off. Some laws were passed saying that the criminal's hand could be cut off as punishment.

An extract from a modern textbook.

SOURCE H

A drawing from 1613, showing two people being punished in the pillory for pretending to be fortune tellers.

Key words

Plead To say whether you are innocent or guilty when you are charged with a crime.

Peine forte et dure A French phrase meaning 'strong and hard pain'.

If person accused of a crime refused to **plead**, he could not be found guilty and so his property could not be taken by the government. But the penalty for this was **peine forte et dure**. The victim would lie and have weights piled up on them until they died.

In 1605 Walter Calverley killed two of his sons and his wife. He intended to kill another son, Henry, but was arrested. Calverley refused to plead. He wanted Henry to inherit his property. Calverley was pressed to death.

In 1672 Henry Jones refused to plead and was sentenced to be pressed. His agony began on Saturday, the day after he appeared in court, and he did not die until midday on Monday.

An extract from a modern book on punishment and torture.

TASKS...

1 Look at sources E to I. Why do you think so many Tudor punishments were carried out in public?

2 You are a judge in the reign of Elizabeth I. Decide what punishment you might have given to:

   a) A lord who had planned to assassinate Elizabeth I.

   b) A Catholic priest who was found in hiding.

   c) A labourer who stole from a shop.

   d) An unemployed woman who tricked a servant into giving her some of her mistress's silver.

   e) A shopkeeper who refused to plead when accused of murdering his wife.

   Read your decisions to the court (the rest of the class) explaining why your punishments fit the crimes.

Plenary

Write down three questions about torture and punishment that you have answered in this section and three questions you have not answered. Where and how might you find the answers to these questions?

WHY DID CRIME INCREASE IN THE SIXTEENTH AND SEVENTEENTH CENTURIES?

Objectives

By the end of this section you will know:
- why there was so much crime in towns
- what types of crime were common in the Tudor period.

You will be able to:
- complete an activity using evidence from sources.

A homeless person begging in modern-day Europe.

A person begging in the seventeenth century.

Starter

- *Do you think that begging, as shown in Source A, should be a crime?*

- *Why might the man have ended up begging?*

- *What do you think might happen to him in the future?*

- *Do you think that the beggar in Source B should have been treated as a criminal?*

- *Why might he have ended up begging?*

- *What do you think might have happened to him next?*

Why was there so much crime in towns?

TASKS...

1 The list below shows reasons why there might have been a lot of crime in Elizabethan England. Put them in order of importance from the most important to least important cause of crime.

Enclosures put many people out of work.	*Towns were growing quickly.*
When a man was ill or died, his family was often faced with poverty.	*There weren't enough jobs to go round.*
	There was no street lighting in towns or villages.
There was only one Constable in each parish.	*Cruelty to **apprentices** meant that up to 50 per cent of them ran away.*
There was no organised police force.	

2 Can you think of any other reasons why people might have turned to crime? Make a list and again put your reasons in order of importance.

Key words

Apprentice A boy sent to a skilled worker, such as a carpenter, to learn a trade.

What types of crime existed?

As you have seen, Elizabeth I's government was so worried about the problem of beggars that it passed new laws (the Poor Laws) to deal with them. What beggars were actually doing was stealing - they tricked people to get their money. But beggars were only a part of the problem.

Large towns also had pickpockets, burglars and cut-purses, who would steal a man's purse by cutting it from his belt. There were also confidence-tricksters. They persuaded their victims to hand over money by getting them to trust them. Gangs of ex-soldiers even used weapons to hold people up and rob them. Some shopkeepers used faulty weights to give their customers less than they paid for.

SOURCE C

A well-dressed traveller asked for a room and food and drink. He asked for the largest silver bowl in the inn to be filled with drink, lemons and sugar, with a silver spoon to stir it. In the dead of night he got up and took his horse out of the stable, put straw on the ground so that no-one would hear it and took away the bowl, spoon, pillow, beer and bed linen.

A description of a burglary written in 1691.

Shoplifting was common even though the punishment for stealing more than five shillings (25p) was hanging. In coastal towns there was smuggling as well.

There were also many violent crimes including fights. But the most serious crimes were murder and treason - plotting against the government. Anyone involved in these could expect no mercy if they were caught.

SOURCE D

Three months ago I caught a thief who was later executed. He told me that he and two others stayed in an inn for three weeks. During this time they stole twenty fat sheep. They also stopped a poor man from ploughing by stealing his ox.

A Justice of the Peace in Elizabeth I's reign describing the activities of robbers.

SOURCE E

A drawing of a highwayman robbing a tinker at gunpoint in 1664.

There has been a complaint about a dog belonging to Peter Quotes. It steals joints of meat from neighbours' houses. The dog doesn't spoil them but carries them whole to his master's house. This dog makes money for his master, but he is annoying to many people, so his master is fined every time.

An entry from the Southampton Court Records.

TASKS...

1 a) Make a list of crimes described in this section.
   b) Compare your list of crimes with your neighbour's and add any you missed to your list.
2 Put the crimes in order from the most serious to the least serious.
3 What punishment do you think would have gone with each crime?

The popular press

Pamphlets were the Tudor equivalent to news reports on television or in newspapers. The first ones were about religion. But soon people wanted to read about crime and punishment.

SOURCE **G**

A seventeenth-century pamphlet showing execution by hanging.

TASKS...

1 Produce a story board about a crime and its punishment in Tudor England. **WS** Use what you have learned so far to give you ideas for your story board. You will need to show:

- Who the criminal was.
- What sort of crime was committed.
- How the crime was carried out.
- How the criminal was caught.
- How the criminal was punished.

2 In a small group, use one of the story boards to produce a play about a crime and how it was punished in the sixteenth century. You will need to think about:

- Who the criminal is.
- What the crime was.
- How the criminal was caught.
- How the criminal was punished.

3 Draw a poster to explain to poor people in the sixteenth century that crime doesn't pay. Remember that not many poor people could read, so there will not be much point in using words on your poster. Your pictures will also have to be very clear.

Plenary

In groups, talk for 60 seconds on 'Crime in the sixteenth century'. If you get stuck, someone else will take over. The person speaking at the end of the minute is the winner.

WHY WAS THERE A WITCH-CRAZE IN THE SEVENTEENTH CENTURY?

WHY DID PEOPLE BELIEVE IN WITCHES?

Objectives

By the end of this section you will know:
- why many people were afraid of witches
- what events were linked to witchcraft.

Starter

A modern artist's impression of the trial of Tracy Smith.

The scene above shows a modern courtroom. A woman, Tracy Smith, is accused of crimes against her neighbour, Sarah Wilson. The lawyer for the prosecution is summing up his evidence for the jury.

Read Source A.

Did Tracy Smith do those things to Sarah Wilson? If you were on the jury, what would you believe? Why?

Make a list of the evidence you thought about, for example, that Tracy Smith had rat poison and Sarah Wilson's cat had been poisoned.

Now discuss your list with your neighbour.

The defendant, Tracy Smith, lived near the victim, Sarah Wilson, and used to baby-sit for her. One day they fell out. Tracy asked to borrow some money and Sarah said no. A witness said Tracy was very angry and shouted 'I'll get you for that'. From that time, things went wrong for Sarah. Her car was badly scratched. Rubbish appeared in her garden. Her cat was poisoned. She got threatening telephone calls from a woman with an accent like Tracy's. These calls came from a public phone at the end of Tracy Smith's street. Her fingerprints were found on the door of Sarah's car and a box of rat poison was found in her garage.

I put it to you, members of the jury, that Tracy Smith has harassed Sarah Wilson. You should find her guilty.

The prosecution sums up its evidence for the jury.

Why did people believe that witchcraft caused bad things to happen to them?

In the sixteenth and seventeenth centuries there was a 'witch-craze'. Thousands of people were killed for being witches. What caused people to believe in witchcraft and to think that witches could do them serious harm?

TASKS...

1 As you read the following information, make a list of the reasons why people believed in witches. Highlight your reasons with different colours.
   - Use one colour if your reason is because of fear or superstition.
   - Use another colour if it is because of religion.
   - Use a third colour if it is because people didn't know much about science.
   - You could highlight some in more than one colour.

Wise women, or witches?

Little was known about health or medicine. In small villages there were always women who knew how to use herbs to make medicines. They often helped when someone was ill or having a baby, and they were usually called 'wise women'.

Unexplained events

Sometimes people living on their own seemed odd - perhaps they talked to their animals. In every village things happened and people could not explain why. Cows died. Babies suffered from fits. People died suddenly from disease. No one knew how these diseases were spread or how to cure them.

People did not know very much about how the natural world worked. Mental illness frightened people. It was not understood. If a person acted in a strange way they thought it was an evil spirit in them.

The role of religion

As you discovered in Chapters 1, 2 and 4, people were very religious at this time. When they went to church they were told about evil, the devil and hell. Plagues like the Black Death were blamed on people's wickedness. It was thought God had sent a punishment, or the Devil was to blame.

💡 Why do you think people were so frightened of witches?

TASKS...

1 Study the following evidence about why people were accused of witchcraft.

a) Make a list showing all the events which were blamed on witchcraft.

b) Opposite each one, write any natural or scientific explanations you can think of for what happened.

SOURCE B

Sometimes one side of their bodies didn't work. Sometimes they would be sore over their whole bodies, so they couldn't bear anyone to touch them. At other times they couldn't hear. At other times they couldn't see or speak. At other times they would faint. Sometimes they would cough and bring up a lot of phlegm containing crooked pins. Once they coughed up a nail with a very broad head.

Amy Duny was accused of putting a spell on 11-year-old Elizabeth Pacy and her sister. This is what was said at her trial in 1645.

SOURCE C

She said that the devil came to her in the shape of a little dog. She said it told her to leave God and follow him ... She called her devil Bunnie. Bunnie pushed Thomas Gardler out of a window, and he fell into a cesspool. She gave some of her blood to the Devil. She said that Jane Holt, Elizabeth Harris and Joan Argoll were her partners. Her devil told her that Elizabeth Harris cursed the boat of John Woofcott.

Joan Williford's confession, 1645. She was sentenced to death.

SOURCE D

She said that Isabel asked her for some milk but she said no. Later she met Isabel and was afraid of her. She was then sick and hurt so much she could not stand. The next day she was suddenly pinched on her thigh with four fingers and a thumb. She was sick, but soon after got better.

Jane Wilkinson gave this evidence against Isabel Robey at a trial of witches in Lancaster in 1612.

WHY WAS THERE A WITCH-CRAZE?

SOURCE E

Even kings and queens believed in witches:

- Henry IV accused his step-mother of making him ill.
- King Richard III accused a woman of plotting to overthrow him by using witchcraft.
- Henry VIII accused Anne Boleyn of bewitching him into marrying her.
- James I accused a woman of causing a storm to wreck his ship. He was so worried about witchcraft that he even wrote a book about it called *Demonology*. He said that witches should be hanged.

If the rulers of the country believed in the power of witchcraft, then ordinary people were likely to believe in it too.

A modern historian writing about witchcraft.

SOURCE F

People said that witches caused all sorts of unpleasant things to happen. These included when:

- animals died
- people had accidents or died suddenly
- beer went off or butter wouldn't churn
- people had strange pains
- crops failed
- ships were wrecked
- children behaved oddly or said strange things, or marks appeared on their bodies.

An extract from a modern history book.

TASKS...

1 Make a poster warning people how to tell if witches are at work. Remember that not many people could read then so use pictures and not many words. **WS**

Plenary

What have you learned so far about witchcraft? Explain it in just one or two sentences. See whether your neighbour thinks the same things are important.

Discuss your ideas in a group and bullet point the five most important facts or ideas.

HOW WERE WITCHES IDENTIFIED?

By the end of this section you will understand:
- how people could tell if someone was a witch
- how people thought witches acted.

Starter

Look at the cartoon of the witch. Write down everything you can see in the picture which tells you that the person shown is a witch. Discuss your reasons with a neighbour.

A modern cartoon of a stereotypical witch.

Key words

Stereotypical A view of someone or something which relies on a common assumption, for example, Frenchmen wear striped jumpers and berets.

What did people think a witch was like?

Most people agreed about how to tell a witch. Books were written about it.

As you read the following descriptions of witches, list the things that would tell you if a person was a witch.

Witches are old, with weak brains. They are very sad, and the devil tricks them into believing he is their friend, so they do strange things. Our witches are clever and cunning.

A description of witches in the early seventeenth century, by William Perkins, a Cambridge preacher

Familiars were thought to be evil spirits that belonged to the witch and helped her to bewitch people. Familiars usually looked like animals. Remember that old people, who were often lonely, turned to pets for friendship.

This drawing of witches with their familiars was made after the Chelmsford witch trials of 1589.

Key words

Familiars Imps or demons which followed a witch around.
Supernatural Not of this world.

People thought that witches could do **supernatural** things:

- They could make storms or cause plagues, or crops to fail. People did not know the real reasons for these things.
- They could fly on broomsticks. Old women often made their own ointments. Some of these could give a feeling of rising up.
- They enjoyed sex. The Church said that not having sex was a good thing.
- They could go to sea in a sieve. Obviously this needed serious magic!

A modern historian.

A MOST
Certain, Strange, and true Difcovery of a

VVITCH.

Being taken by fome of the Parliament Forces, as fhe was ftanding on a fmall planck-board and fayling on it over the River of *Newbury*:

Together with the ftrange and true manner of her death, with the propheticall words and fpeeches fhe vfed at the fame time.

A seventeenth-century pamphlet about a witch.

How did people know so much about witches?

People liked to read about mysteries and horror. Now that the printing press had been invented, lots of books were produced cheaply. Although many people were **illiterate,** stories of witch trials were very popular. Short pamphlets were printed about what the witches had done and how they were punished.

Key words

Illiterate Unable to read.

TASKS...

1 Imagine that you are a printer in 1645. People want to know about witches who have been caught. Printing these stories can make you money.

   a) Produce a pamphlet about a witch trial in 1645. Include a lot of information and make it interesting. **WS**
   - Start by designing the front page.
   - Draw and describe the witch. Use the information you have learned. Think about what witches looked like. How did they behave?
   - Write about what was said in court about the witch.

   b) As you learn more about witchcraft, add more information to your pamphlet.

Plenary

Show the front page of your pamphlet to your group. Explain what you have tried to show.

WHY WERE WITCHFINDERS SO BUSY IN ENGLAND IN THE 1640s?

Objectives

By the end of this section you will find out:
- why witchfinders were invited to villages to catch witches
- what made people so frightened of witches
- how witchfinders made people confess to being witches.

You will be able to:
- explain how the problems people faced made them believe in witches.

Starter

In groups, take turns to list reasons for suspecting someone of witchcraft. Before you add your reason, repeat what everybody else has said. For example, 'A woman might be called a witch because someone's cows had died'. 'A woman might be called a witch because someone's cows had died and because people were afraid of the Devil.' and so on. How many reasons can your group remember?

Why were people so worried about witchcraft in England in the 1640s?

TASKS...

1 Look at the nine events and facts listed at the top of page 151. Which of them might have made people believe in witches in the 1640s and 1650s. Put them in order of importance. Start with the most important. **WS**

2 Compare your list with others in the class. Discuss it until you have decided the five most important reasons.

| The Civil War had made people scared and uncertain. | It was difficult to get news and information in country areas. | People were poorer - villages had lost crops and workers in the Civil War. |

| England had become Protestant. The Catholic Church said it protected people against magic. | People were confused about what was happening to their world. | The government was a long way away in London. It kept changing and no-one knew what was happening. |

| In the new Protestant Church the priest didn't have special powers to protect people - he was just an ordinary man. | Puritans believed the devil was trying to make people follow him. | Country people were very superstitious. |

Why did people invite witchfinders to their village?

Witchfinders told villagers they came from the government. This was not true. They gained people's trust by the 'discovery of witches'.

Matthew Hopkins began his career as a witchfinder by making a one-legged woman called Elizabeth Clarke confess to being a witch. Hopkins kept her awake for three days. Clarke eventually confessed and named another five witches. Local people were frightened that there were witches in their area.

SOURCE A

A seventeenth-century illustration showing Matthew Hopkins and Elizabeth Clarke (both of the witches) with her familiars.

Which parts of Source A do you think people would have been most worried by? Why?

Do you think that Source A shows what really happened? Why?

If Source A does not show what really happened, how can it still be a useful piece of evidence for historians?

SOURCE B

Greetings, your Worship,

I have received a letter to come to your town to search for witches. But I hear your minister is against us. I will come to hear his views. I have heard a minister in Suffolk speak against the discovery of witches. He soon changed his mind. I shall visit your town soon.

Your servant,

Matthew Hopkins

A letter written in 1645 by Hopkins to a Justice of the Peace in Essex.

TASKS...

1   **a)** The Protestant minister in Source B didn't like witchfinders. Can you think why?

b) Write the speech this minister might have made in church, explaining why Hopkins should not be invited to the town. Use the information you have learned. Think about why people were worried at this time. **WS**

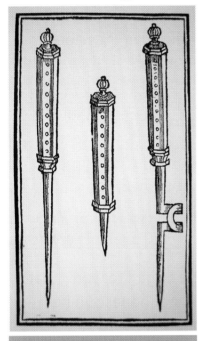

SOURCE C

Why were witchfinders so successful?

TASKS...

1 Using information from Sources C to H, make a list of how witchfinders got confessions. Explain why each one would work.

2 When you have finished, look at the pamphlet you started about a witchcraft trial. Add a description of how the witchfinder got his evidence about the witches.

💡 *What do you think the objects in Source C are used for? Write down possible answers.*

Tools used by a witchfinder.

SOURCE D

The witchfinder would keep his victims awake, until they would admit anything. The victim would usually be naked. Her pets would come to her, having sniffed their way there. This showed that they were in fact her imps. The victim would be flung into the water, tied hand and foot, and left to God's judgement. To float was a sign that you worked for the Devil. To sink was to prove you were innocent.

A historian, writing in 1981, describes how witchfinders stopped victims from sleeping and then used the method called 'swimming' to test them.

SOURCE E

They kept him awake for several nights, and ran him around the room until he was out of breath. They did this for several days and nights until he was hardly aware of what he said or did. They swam him but that was not a true test. Honest people were swum at the same time and they swam as well as he did.

A report of the treatment of John Lowes, a Suffolk vicar, who was tried for witchcraft at Bury St Edmunds in 1615.

WHY WAS THERE A WITCH-CRAZE?

Witches Apprehended, Examined and Executed, for notable villanies by them committed both by Land and Water.

With a strange and most true triall how to know whether a woman be a Witch or not.

Printed at London for *Edward Marchant*, and are to

A pamphlet showing the practice of 'swimming' a witch.

A bishop told how one old woman was forced to confess that she had an 'imp' called 'Nan'. She didn't know what she had confessed and only had a chicken that she sometimes called 'Nan'. The witchfinders kept these poor people without food or sleep. To stop the torture they told tales of their pets.

An opinion of Matthew Hopkins' methods written in 1645.

Some people began to worry that Hopkins was not honest. So he wrote a pamphlet called *The Discovery of Witches* to answer some of the questions usually put to him. (see Source H).

Question: Once the Devil's mark has been found, why must the victims be kept awake? This makes them say anything.
Answer: If they were kept awake they would call their familiars to help them.

Question: Why did you force them to keep walking until their feet were sore and they confessed?
Answer: They were only walked to keep them awake.

Question: Why did you use 'swimming' – it is inhumane and illegal.
Answer: King James said that this was a sure test for a witch. Many ministers (whom I respect) have said swimming is wrong, so I don't do it any more.

An extract from *The Discovery of Witches*, written by Matthew Hopkins in 1647.

How were convicted witches punished?

Hopkins may have been involved in the trials of some 200 women between 1645 and 1647. About half were sentenced to hang.

In the eighteenth century fewer people were executed for witchcraft. Sometimes 'witches' were imprisoned or put in the pillory.

TASKS...

1 Using the information you have read in this section, complete your pamphlet. Describe what happened to the witches. The objects on page 153 are 'witchpricker's knives'. They were used to prick the skin in order to find a special witch's mark. You could illustrate your pamphlet with a drawing like this.

2 Swap pamphlets with a partner. Make a list of good points that your partner has made and also anything they have missed out. How could you make your pamphlet better?

Plenary

If you could interview Matthew Hopkins, what three questions would you ask him?

WHY DID THE NUMBER OF WITCHCRAFT TRIALS DECLINE AFTER THE 1640s?

Objectives

By the end of this section you will understand:
- why the number of witchcraft trials went down after the 1640s
- how progress in science meant that fewer people believed in witches.

You will be able to:
- find information from several sources to answer a question.

Starter

Brainstorm a list of reasons why you don't believe in witchcraft.

Why were people becoming less superstitious?

There were some important scientific discoveries and inventions in the seventeenth century.

- William Harvey discovered that blood flowed round the body.
- The printing press meant more information was available.
- People realised that the earth moved round the sun and not the other way round.

- The Royal Society was set up to help scientists in their work.
- The first microscopes were used.
- Telescopes were used to look at the moon.
- Isaac Newton explained gravity.

TASKS...

1 Why do you think these changes might stop people believing in witchcraft?

2 Look back at your list of reasons why you don't believe in witchcraft. How many of your reasons are to do with science?

TASKS...

3 On pages 150–1 you listed reasons why people were worried about witches in the 1640s. Can you match up the problems of the 1640s below with the changes which might have solved them by 1700? **‹WS›**

Problems in the 1640s

The Civil War had made people scared and uncertain.

Puritans believed the Devil was trying to make people follow him.

It was difficult to get news and information in country areas.

People were poor - villages had lost crops and workers in the Civil War.

England had become Protestant. The Catholic Church said it protected people against magic.

Changes by 1700

Protestantism was no longer new. Now Catholicism seemed old-fashioned.

Villages had long recovered from the Civil War. People had settled down and were better off.

There had been a secure government for a long time by 1700.

Transport and communications were better. Country areas were not so cut off from the big towns.

Puritans didn't control country villages any more.

Why were there fewer witchcraft trials in the eighteenth century?

After the 1640s there were fewer and fewer trials for witchcraft.

- People understood much more about science - even ordinary people.
- Many machines were invented. People could see that there was no magic in using steam power to make a pump work.

- There were few plagues and no famines.
- Religion was not as violent.
- There was peace in the country - people were not fighting each other any more.

TASKS...

1 Now you are ready to answer the big question about witchcraft:

'Why was there a "witch-craze" in the mid-seventeenth century?' **WS**

Write paragraphs to explain the answer to this question.

First make a plan to show what you are going to include in each paragraph.

You could use a table like this:

1. People were thought to be witches if…	2. Times were dangerous and worrying.	3. Witchfinders made things worse.	4. Victims often confessed to being witches.	5. Many people were found guilty of being witches.
Old women were often suspected because… When strange things happened…	There had been a civil war which turned their lives… After the war Puritans ran the country and they…	They made people worry about witches because…	This was because witchfinders…	Their punishment was… The way this affected other people was that…

Plenary

Discuss with a partner the plan you made for answering the big question.

💡 Who has made more points in each paragraph?

💡 What have you left out?

THEME: SOCIAL LIFE

CONCLUSION

At the start of this theme you probably thought that living in Tudor and Stuart times was very dull and boring. Now you can see that their lives were hard work and that they often faced danger but people still had time to go out and enjoy themselves.

People's lives changed a lot between 1500 and 1750. There were changes in science and the arts, in jobs, leisure activities and even in the food people ate.

To build up a fuller picture of the times, plot on your timeline important events and changes in the lives of ordinary people, for example the witch craze of the 1640s. Also, along the bottom of the timeline, make a list of threats and opportunities which faced people in their everyday struggle to survive.

An example has been done for you below.

Ruler	*Charles I/Parliament*
Main Religion	*Protestant*
Political Events	*Civil War*
Changes in people's lives	*Witch trials, 1640s*
Threats and Opportunities	*Threats: Puritan rule*

THEME: EXTERNAL RELATIONS

INTRODUCTION

Between 1500 and 1750 British people started to look outwards past Europe to the rest of the world. English sailors such as Sir Francis Drake sailed across seas which had not been mapped. They explored parts of the world which Europeans did not know at that time. They were looking for new lands, for fame and for gold. At the same time, small groups of English people were leaving their homes to find a better life in America. The most famous were the Pilgrim Fathers.

Back at home England tried to control Scotland, Wales and Ireland. The Protestants and Catholics in Ireland hated each other. In the 1650s many men, women and children on both sides were killed. English actions in Ireland did not help the people to get on better.

In 1603 James VI of Scotland became King James I of England as well but England and Scotland stayed separate countries. It was only in 1707 that they united and England gained control of Scotland. However, the Scots still rebelled against English rule in 1715 and 1745.

England's growing power also meant rivalry with France. In Elizabeth I's reign (1558-1603), when England had become Protestant, there was conflict with Spain. King Philip II of Spain sent a huge fleet to invade England in 1588 but it was defeated.

In the two hundred and fifty years between 1500 and 1750 England became an important power in the world.

TIMELINE
1500–1750

1511–14, 1522–5, 1544–6
King Henry VIII is at war against France.

1557–9 War against France during the reigns of Mary I and Elizabeth I.

1577–80 Sir Francis Drake sails round the world.

1587 Elizabeth I executes Mary, Queen of Scots.

1588 Philip II of Spain sends 130 ships to invade England, but the Armada fails.

1595 Sir Walter Raleigh sails to South America.

1600 The East India Company is formed.

1642–9 During the English Civil War the Irish Catholics support Charles I.

1655 Jamaica in the West Indies is captured by the English.

1664 The English take New Amsterdam in North America and rename it New York.

1683 Pennsylvania is founded in North America.

1689 James II lands in Ireland and raises an army of Irish Catholics.

1690 William III lands in Ireland and defeats James II at the Battle of the Boyne.

1692 The massacre at Glencoe.

1707 The Act of Union formally unites England and Scotland.

1750 Britain gains control of most of North America's east coast.

10

WHY DID ENGLAND HAVE ENEMIES ABROAD IN THE SIXTEENTH CENTURY?

WHY WERE THE ENGLISH SO OFTEN AT WAR IN THE SIXTEENTH CENTURY?

Objectives

In this section you will look at:
• why there were so many wars between England and France.

Starter

💡 *What differences do you notice between the map showing Europe in the early sixteenth century and the map of Europe today? Is there anything that is the same?*

Key
- ■ Lands of the Holy Roman Emperor Charles V
- -- Boundary of the Holy Roman Empire. This was made up of about 300 small states; their rulers were under the influence of Emperor Charles V.

Europe in the early sixteenth century.

A map of Europe today.

Relations between England and France in the sixteenth century

For hundreds of years England and France had been rivals. There were many wars between the two countries. The longest war was the so-called Hundred Years' War. This actually lasted from 1337 to 1453.

The Tudor kings and queens kept up their claim to the French throne. They showed this by putting the badge of the French kings on their coat of arms (see below).

English monarchs also wanted to keep the balance of power in Europe. They did not want one country to become too powerful as it might invade England. England often sided with other countries to reduce the power of France.

The ambitions of Henry VIII

Henry VII had tried to keep the peace with France through clever **diplomacy** and by marrying his daughter Mary to the king of France.

But Henry VIII wanted to take back English land that had been lost during the Hundred Years' War.

💡 What do you think a diplomat is?

TASKS...

As you read the information on pages 163–5, try to decide why England went to war with France. Choose from the following reasons:

- To win new lands.
- To take back lands which had been held by English kings in the past.
- To solve the problem of Scotland.
- To protect England from attack.
- To make sure that other countries did not become too powerful.
- To win the monarch glory.
- To make sure that other countries did not take over or threaten English trade.
- To defend the English religion or to force the religion of England on the other country.

The Tudor royal coat of arms showing the badge of the French kings.

Key words

Diplomacy Working at keeping good relations with another country.

Henry went to war against France for personal glory and not for the interests of his country.

The historian G.R. Elton writing in 1955.

Henry VIII's task was to solve the Scottish problem. He said the war was needed to bring Scotland under English control.

The historian M.D. Palmer writing in 1971.

After the Reformation under Henry VIII (see Chapter 1), England broke with the Roman Catholic Church. Henry became the Head of the Church in England and was no longer 'Defender of the Faith', a title given to him by the Pope. The more England moved towards the Protestant religion the greater the rivalry with France, the leading Catholic country.

France and Scotland were closely linked. The two countries often allied with one another in the sixteenth century. War with one usually meant war with the other.

In 1512 Henry VIII joined with the Holy Roman Emperor to fight a war against France. He was let down by the emperor who made peace with France behind Henry's back. The war cost a lot of money. By the time it was over, Henry had spent all the money left by his father.

The Field of Cloth of Gold

In 1520 Henry went to France to talk to his enemy, the French king, Francis I. The two kings met on the Field of Cloth of Gold. The meeting became known as this because the kings met in one of many tents made of gold cloth. The two men talked of a possible **alliance** between the two countries.

💡 Can you think of a recent example of an alliance?

Key words

Alliance An agreement between two or more countries to help one another, usually in a war.

The 'Field of Cloth of Gold', 1520. This was painted around 20 years after the event. It shows several different scenes.

The meeting at the Field of Cloth of Gold did not lead to friendship between England and France. Within two years, England was at war with France again. This time Henry fought alongside the Holy Roman Emperor, Charles (see map on page 162). Then, in 1525, Henry swapped sides and joined France to fight against the Emperor. He changed sides because he was disappointed with his alliance with the Emperor, who was also the nephew and supporter of Henry's wife, Catherine of Aragon, from whom he now wanted a divorce (see Chapter 1).

After this, there were no more wars between the two countries for nearly 20 years.

In 1544 Henry's army invaded France. The following year there was a sea-battle between the French and the English off the south coast of England. The French lost.

TASKS...

1 **a)** Look back at the list of reasons why England went to war with France.

   b) Put them in order of importance with the most important first. Use a diamond shape to put together your answer:

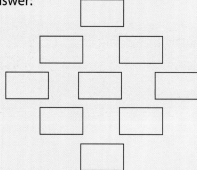

2 **a)** Draw a living graph to plot how relations between England and France changed.

   b) Label each of the main events along the bottom of the graph. Put a cross on the graph to show how the relationship between the countries changed – was it good, very good, bad or even very bad?

EXTENSION TASK

3 Use your graph to help you write a paragraph to summarise why relations between England and France changed between 1511 and 1550.

Plenary

Which of the statements below are true? Which are false?

1 England was often at war with France during Henry VIII's reign.

2 The meeting between Henry VIII and Francis I was known as the 'Field of Cloth'.

3 England went to war to take new lands from France.

4 Henry's wars against France were very successful.

5 Henry's wars against France were very expensive.

6 Diplomacy means two countries agree to help each other.

Make up two statements of your own about relations between England and France.

Try them out on someone else in the class.

WHAT HAPPENED TO ENGLAND'S RELATIONS WITH SPAIN UNDER ELIZABETH I?

Objectives

In this section you will try to work out:
• why relations between Spain and England became so bad that Spain tried to invade England in 1588.

I write to tell you about my terrible time on board ship. The sea was very rough and we were all very sea sick.

Our cabins are dark and evil-smelling. For sport there are fine fights of cockroaches, and very good rat-hunting. The lice are huge.

Our food consists of broken biscuits and a few beef bones. At mealtimes, the ship's crew come rushing to eat those poor bones. Men and women, young and old, clean and dirty, are all mixed up together. The people around you throw up or go to the toilet while you are having your breakfast.

To go to the toilet, you have to hang out over the sea like a cat-burglar clinging to a wall.

The worst is wishing for something to drink. You are in the middle of the sea, surrounded by water, but they give the water out in thimbles, and all the time you are dying of thirst from eating dried beef and food pickled in salt.

A Spaniard, Eugenio de Salazar, sailed across the Atlantic in 1573 in a small ship. This is part of a letter that he wrote.

Starter

 What can you learn from Source A about life at sea at this time? You could make a list or even draw a picture to show this.

A historical mystery

Fifteen years after his journey across the Atlantic, Eugenio de Salazar sailed on one of the ships of the Spanish Armada to invade England.

• Why did Spain and England go to war?

• Who was most to blame for the war, Elizabeth I or Philip II?

Look at pages 168–9 for help.

TASKS...

1 Re-order the following statements to help you understand why Spain and England went to war and who was to blame. **WS**

a English privateers attacked Spanish treasure ships.

b In 1559 Philip II of Spain asked Elizabeth I to marry him, but she said no.

c Spain was a Catholic country and England was Protestant. The English were afraid that Philip would make them become Catholics.

d The Spanish tried to get English Catholics to murder Elizabeth I and make Mary, Queen of Scots, Queen of England.

e Spain controlled much of Central and South America. It wanted to keep all of the trade with this area for Spain. When English merchants tried to trade with the Spanish colonies, it led to the Battle of San Juan de Ulua in 1568.

f After the Battle of San Juan de Ulua, Englishmen such as John Hawkins and Francis Drake attacked Spanish ships and colonies. Queen Elizabeth I got some of the profits from these attacks.

g In 1587 Elizabeth I had Mary, Queen of Scots executed. This made Philip II angry.

h The Netherlands belonged to Philip II of Spain. Protestants in the Netherlands rebelled against their Catholic ruler. Elizabeth I supported the rebels and, in 1585, sent an army to help them.

i In 1569 Elizabeth I thought about marrying the heir to the French throne, Philip II's enemy.

j In 1587 Francis Drake destroyed 30 Spanish warships and ships carrying supplies, which were ready to invade England.

k In 1581 Elizabeth I passed a law banning the Catholic religion in England.

l The rulers of the Turkish empire were enemies of Spain. In 1580, England signed a trade treaty with Turkey.

m In Spain, there were a few Protestants. Philip ordered Protestants to be killed.

n In 1568 Elizabeth I captured three Spanish treasure ships.

o In 1580 Philip II invaded Portugal. Elizabeth I promised to help Portugal attack Philip.

p Dutch pirates attacked Spanish ships. Elizabeth I allowed them to use English ports.

q France was an enemy of Spain. In 1581, the Duke of Anjou led a French army to help the Dutch. He signed a marriage treaty with Elizabeth I.

r English traders took slaves to sell to Spain's colonies in America. Philip II had ordered that only Spanish merchants could trade with its colonies.

Key words

Colonies Foreign lands settled and ruled by people for the benefit of their homeland.

TASKS...

2 Below are drawings of Elizabeth I and Philip II.

Sketch the drawings in your book:

- Put each of the statements next to the rulers to show who was to blame.
- Put any statements that show both were to blame between the two drawings.

3 Write an answer to the question:

Who was more to blame for the war between England and Spain, Elizabeth or Philip?

Here is a writing frame to help you:

In 1588, England and Spain went to war.

Philip II was to blame because ...

Elizabeth was to blame because ...

I think ...   was most to blame because ...

💡 Name two countries that used to be British colonies.

Plenary

Using IT, write a headline for either a Spanish or English newspaper, showing who you think was to blame for the war between England and Spain.

SHOULD THE DEFEAT OF THE ARMADA BE REWRITTEN?

Objectives

In this section you will:
- see whether the traditional view of the defeat of the Armada fits with the evidence
- re-write history.

Starter

The Newcastle Gazette   **19 November 2002**

Newcastle hammer Saints 2–1!

Newcastle's title hopes looked rosy after destroying Southampton 2–1 yesterday in a performance that had everything. Despite having only forty per cent of the possession and only 3 attempts on goal to the Saints' ten, Newcastle showed their superiority in the 21st minute when Shearer headed into the top corner of the net. Claims that he was offside were dismissed by the referee.

Southampton were unable to convert any of their seven corners and they had four separate appeals for penalties turned down. When Bellamy went past Bridge and nutmegged Jones for Newcastle's second the game was all over. It took a very muddled goal in the 89th minute to restore some pride to the Southampton team. Comments that the referee was biased were clearly unfounded. The Saints weren't robbed – their finishing was simply poor.

An imaginary Premiership football match.

Read the newspaper article.

 Was Newcastle lucky to win? What evidence can you find?

 Why do you think the newspaper gives this interpretation of the match?

 Now re-write this account basing your version only on the facts and evidence shown in the article.

We have similar problems with views of past events. They are often written to favour one side.

The Armada: what actually happened?

Below is a traditional account of the English defeat of the Spanish Armada.

A traditional view of the defeat of the Armada, by Historian A

Philip II of Spain sent a powerful fleet of ships known as the Armada to England. The Armada was to clear the English Channel of Elizabeth I's ships and then take the king's army from the Netherlands to England.

The Armada sailed to England in July 1588. It was made up of 130 ships and was much bigger than the English navy. Philip chose the Duke of Medina Sidonia, who knew little about the sea, to command the fleet.

The Armada formed the shape of a crescent, making it difficult to attack. The odds were very much against England. It took over a week for the Spanish fleet to sail up the Channel.

Queen Elizabeth was not frightened by the threat from Spain and cheered on her sailors with a speech.

The English ships seemed no match for the huge Spanish ships. On 27 July the Armada anchored near Calais. The commander of the English fleet, Lord Howard, sent eight fireships into the Armada forcing the Spanish ships to sail out into the open sea. The faster English ships were able to attack and sank many of the Spanish ships.

The Duke of Medina Sidonia had to sail home round the coast of Scotland, and many of his ships were lost in storms. Only 60 ships returned home to Spain. The most powerful navy in the world had been defeated by the bravery of the English commander, sailors and queen. Spain never threatened England again.

💡 Why do you think Historian A's version of the defeat of the Armada has been popular in British textbooks?

💡 How accurate is this version of the Armada?

Now look at the evidence provided by Sources A–F.

SOURCE A

The leader of the Armada ought to understand navigation and sea fighting. I know nothing of either. I know none of the officers who are to serve under me and I know nothing of the state of England.

A letter from the Duke of Medina Sidonia to Philip II in 1588.

The Armada, sailing north, ran into storms and had to put into port for repairs. Leaving some ships behind, Medina Sidonia put his fleet to sea again on 12 July, nearly two months after he'd first set sail. The Armada was now 124 ships.

When the two fleets met, the Spaniards were surprised at the size of the English fleet and its skilled sailing. The English were surprised at the skill of the Spanish defensive crescent shape. Its well-armed ships were on the wings, and the slow-moving, unarmed supply ships in the centre.

From a modern school textbook.

A painting of the Armada sailing in a crescent shape as it entered the Channel, 1588.

Six old ships were stuffed full of things for burning. They were let loose, each one with a man on board. The tide brought them very near to the Spanish fleet. The burning ships came so close to the Spanish ships that they had to sail away as quickly as they could. We followed them. There was fight. They lost a dozen or fourteen of their best ships.

A young Englishman, Robert Carey, was on board one of the English ships.

An English painting showing the English fireships attacking the Spanish fleet.

SOURCE F

By 1577, the English navy had modern fighting ships that could easily move about. The ships had lots of cannons (guns) because hand to hand fighting was thought to be out of date. The Spanish ships were designed to ram the enemy. This allowed their soliders to board a ship and fight it out. For this reason they carried twice as many soldiers as sailors. Not only this but the heavy Spanish guns had a far shorter range than the English. The English fleet could hit and damage a Spanish ship before it got close enough to ram the attacker.

From a modern school textbook.

TASKS...

1 Compare the evidence with Historian A's view of the Armada.

   a) In pairs, work out three questions that you would ask about Historian A's view.

   b) Share your questions with another pair and see if you can come up with ten questions.

   c) Which are the most commonly asked questions agreed by the class as a whole?

TASKS...

2 a) Now, check your questions against Historian A's view.

b) Is there anything from the evidence of Historian A that you would question or change? Here are some things to check:
- the size of the fleets
- Medina Sidonia's leadership
- the quality of the English and Spanish ships
- the tactics used by the English.

3 Historians are always re-writing the past. Here's your chance to re-write history. You are Historian B. You have been asked to write about the defeat of the Armada, which could be translated into Spanish and used in Spanish schools. You should include:
- Spanish weaknesses and mistakes
- English strengths
- examples of good luck.

Plenary

Write down five key words that you have learned in this section. Ask someone else in your class to define the word.

11

THE CELTIC FRINGE: WHY WERE THE SCOTS AND IRISH DISCONTENTED IN THE SEVENTEENTH AND EIGHTEENTH CENTURIES?

DROGHEDA: WAS CROMWELL A WAR CRIMINAL?

Objectives

In this section you will look at the evidence and decide:
- whether the **massacre** at Drogheda was a justifiable act of war
- whether Cromwell was a war criminal.

Starter

💡 *What is happening in Source A?*

💡 *Do you think these events happened exactly as shown here? Why?*

Key words
Massacre The killing of a group of people.

SOURCE **A**

Driuinge Men Women & children by hund: reds vpon Briges & casting them into Riuers, who drowned not were killed with poles & shot with muskets.

A Protestant drawing showing the killing of Irish Protestants by Catholics in 1641.

In 1641 an Irish Rebellion took place when Irish Catholics feared Parliament would pass anti-Catholic laws and attacked Protestants. However, the massacre had not been planned in advance.

Background to Drogheda

- During the English Civil War (1642–9) the Irish Catholics fought against Parliament. They wanted Charles I's son to become King of England.

- In 1649 Charles I was executed. Oliver Cromwell, a Puritan, became leader of the new Republic (a government without a monarch).

- By 1649 most of Ireland was controlled by the Irish Catholics. Cromwell wanted to gain control of Ireland.

- The leader of the Irish Catholics went to France to get money and arms.

- Cromwell landed in Ireland and went straight to Drogheda.

Different interpretations

Cromwell's army surrounded the town of Drogheda. The people inside refused to surrender. When his soldiers broke into the town, they killed about 3000 people.

There are two views – interpretations – of what happened.

Interpretation 1	Interpretation 2
This view says that what Cromwell did was wrong.	*This view says that Cromwell acted according to the rules of war at the time.*

TASKS...

1   Look at Sources B-J on pages 177–8.

   a) Which sources agree with the first view (interpretation 1)?

   b) Which sources agree with the second view (interpretation 2)?

For no reason you massacred the English. You did not care who you killed, man or woman, adult or child.

Cromwell told Irish priests that Catholics should be punished for the 'massacres' of Protestants in 1641.

There are two important seventeenth-century rules of warfare you need to know about:

- A successful army could give 'quarter' to the enemy. This meant the enemy would be shown mercy they surrendered and gave up their weapons.
- If an attacking army broke into a town and the people did not surrender, they could all be killed.

From a modern history textbook.

Key words

Mass The Roman Catholic Church service.

A cartoon of 1649 showing St George, the patron saint of England. He is dressed as one of Cromwell's soldiers, trampling on the Irish dragon.

I do not believe that people should have the freedom to carry out **Mass**. It will not be allowed.

Cromwell's views on the Catholic religion, 1650.

Our army came to Drogheda. I asked the people of the town to surrender. When they refused, our guns beat down the walls. The next day, after some fighting, we entered the town. Several of the enemy retreated into Mill Mount. Our men were ordered by me to kill them. I also ordered them to kill any people in the town who had weapons. In the church almost 1000 people were killed. I think that we killed in all about 2000 men. This is God's judgement on our enemy who killed so many innocent people. It will save lives in the future.

From a letter written by Cromwell, after Drogheda, to the House of Commons.

Cromwell's soldiers promised not to kill anyone who put down their weapons. But when they had all in their power, the words 'No quarter' went round.

From a letter written by the Irish Catholic leader, 29 September 1649.

The soldiers threw down their arms on an offer of quarter. The enemy entered Mill Mount. They killed every soldier and every Irish person.

From a letter written by the Duke of Clarendon in 1668. He was in France with the son of Charles I at the time of the events at Drogheda. He was a friend of the Irish Catholic leader.

For the Irish, the way the revolt was crushed was the most important thing. Cromwell said that the massacre would save lives in the future. But in the long run it helped to make bitterness. And that caused far more blood to be spilt.

From a history of Ireland written in 1956.

When the people hid in the churches Cromwell's soldiers followed them up the towers. They held children in front of them as shields. Then they went down into the basement of the churches to kill the women.

An Englishman who saw what happened at Drogheda.

TASKS...

Look at Sources B–J.

1 Which view do you agree with?

2 Write an answer to the following question:

*Was Cromwell a **war criminal** because of what he did at Drogheda?*

Here is a writing frame to help you.

> Sources ... show that Cromwell was not a war criminal. This is because ...
>
> Other sources, such as ... show that he was a war criminal because ...
>
> I believe he was/was not a war criminal because ...

Key words

War criminal Someone who has carried out acts against humanity that break the rules of warfare.

Plenary

You are trying to find out the truth about Drogheda. You have the chance to question Oliver Cromwell.

- Think of two key questions to ask him.
- Share these questions with someone else in your class. Try to come up with five questions.
- Now try your questions on someone in your class, who will act as Oliver Cromwell.

WHAT CHANGES TOOK PLACE IN IRELAND IN THE 1680s AND 1690s?

In this section, you will find out about:

- what conflicts there were between Catholics and Protestants in the seventeenth century
- how changes in Ireland affected Irish Catholic in the 1680s and 1690s.

Starter

Protestant marchers in Northern Ireland remember the Battle of the Boyne.

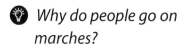 *Why do people go on marches?*

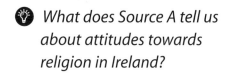 *What does Source A tell us about attitudes towards religion in Ireland?*

James II: a Catholic king

- In 1685 King Charles II died. His Catholic brother, James, became King James II.

- James put Catholics into the important jobs in the army, universities and civil service.

- Catholics in Ireland were given freedom of worship.

- In 1688 James's wife had a son. Many people wondered whether the child was James's baby.

- The English Parliament asked the Protestant Prince William of Orange and his wife Mary (James's daughter) to become king and queen. William came to England and James fled to France.

The siege of Londonderry, 1689

In 1689 James landed in Ireland. He raised an army to fight William.

James and his army marched on Londonderry. The town was being held by Protestant supporters of William. The siege of Londonderry lasted 105 days. No food could get in and about 15,000 Protestants starved to death.

Finally, an English warship came with supplies. The Catholic army gave up and marched away.

The Battle of the Boyne, 1690

- In June 1690 William landed with a huge army in the north of Ireland.

- The armies met at the Battle of the Boyne. James II lost.

- James escaped to France.

- William returned to England. He left his generals to finish putting down the Catholics.

- William then signed a peace treaty with the Catholics. He promised them freedom of worship and fairer treatment.

- In the years that followed, William passed laws against Catholics. They were banned from Parliament, universities and the navy.

- Catholics began to lose land in Ireland.

TASKS...

1 a) Eamonn O'Donnell is an Irish Catholic who lived through the changes in Ireland. How would he feel about the above events?

b) Make a copy of the living graph below and plot his reactions to each event. Explain each one briefly. **WS**

c) Share your findings with a partner. Do you agree with where they have placed the events?

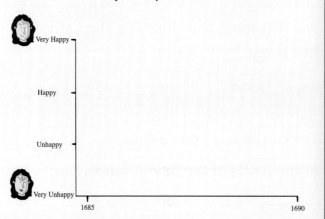

2 Look back at the big banner on page 180 showing the Protestant view of the Battle of the Boyne. Design another banner giving Eamonn O'Donnell's view.

Plenary

Think of two historical words used in this section. Write down the meaning of each word.

Cut out the two words and two meanings. Ask someone else in your class to match the words to the meanings.

WHY DID A MASSACRE TAKE PLACE AT GLENCOE?

Objectives

In this section you will find out:
- why a massacre took place at Glencoe.

Starter

Read Source A.

SOURCE (A)

At five o'clock on the morning of 13 February 1692 two soldiers went into the house of Alexander MacDonald, the leader of the MacDonald **clan**. He got up to welcome them. The soldiers shot him. They also shot and wounded his wife, but she got away. Next day, she died of her injuries.

All along the valley, there was the sound of shots. Clansmen fought with the soldiers to give their wives and children time to escape. As the Campbell soldiers shot their way from house to house, the MacDonalds ran to the hills. Many of them were led over a track across the mountains. Some of them died of the cold. When the soldiers had finished, 38 men, women and children were dead. The houses in the valley were burned to the ground.

A modern account of the Glencoe massacre.

Key words

Clan A group of people with a common family ancestor, such as the MacDonalds and the Campbells.

- *Why were clans important in Scotland?*
- *What do we have instead of clans today?*
- *Think of a newspaper headline for Glencoe.*

SOURCE B

A nineteenth century painting of the massacre of Glencoe.

Solving a mystery

Many television detectives solve murder mysteries by looking at clues and working out what happened. You are going work out the solution to two mystery questions from the evidence which follows.

On 13 February 1692 the leader of the MacDonald clan, Alexander MacDonald, and 37 members of his clan were killed.

💡 Why was Alexander MacDonald killed?

💡 Who was responsible for his death?

Key words

Highlanders People who lived in the far north and west of Scotland.

Lowlanders People who lived in the south and east of Scotland.

Highlands of Scotland

Lowlands of Scotland

N

Highlanders – mostly Catholic

Massacre of Glencoe, 1692 ✕

SCOTLAND

50 km

Inverlochy
Inveraray

Edinburgh

Lowlanders – mostly Protestant

ENGLAND

Where the Scottish Highlanders and Lowlanders lived in 1692.

The Evidence

a Alexander MacDonald decided to take the oath of loyalty to King William III. He arrived at the English fort of Inverlochy on 29 December 1691 but was told that he would have to give the oath to the sheriff at Inverarary, 97 kilometres away.

b Sir John Dalrymple was one of William III's ministers for Scotland. He believed that the Highland clans ought to be made to fear the law.

c William III signed the order for the massacre.

d William III's soldiers carried out the Glencoe massacre.

e The Highland clans were Catholic. They had supported James II in 1689 and had rebelled against William.

f At Glencoe, the Campbells broke the Highland custom of hospitality. This said that the MacDonalds had to welcome the Campbells as their guests and that there must be no fighting.

g Alexander MacDonald did not arrive at Inverarary until 2 January 1692, but the sheriff was away. The sheriff took his oath on 6 January, and wrote a letter to explain why it was late.

h Captain Robert Campbell got the order to kill the MacDonalds while he was their guest.

i The MacDonalds were killed even though they had taken the oath of loyalty to the king.

j William crushed the rebellion of 1689 at the Battle of Dunkeld.

k Sir John Dalrymple said that Alexander MacDonald's oath was too late. He gave the go-ahead for the massacre.

l During the Highland rebellion of 1689, 2000 government soldiers were killed in the pass at Killiecrankie.

m Captain Robert Campbell and 120 Campbell soldiers were sent to live in Glencoe with the MacDonalds. They said that there was no room for them at the fort at Inverlochy.

n There was an inquiry into the massacre. Many people were found guilty but no one was punished.

o After the rebellion of 1689, William III gave £12,000 to the Highlanders. In return, the Highlanders had to swear an oath of loyalty to the king. The oath had to be taken by 1 January 1692.

p Sir John Dalrymple was a member of the Campbell clan.

q The Campbells and MacDonalds were enemies.

r William sent a letter on 11 January 1692 ordering one of his ministers to punish people who had not taken the oath. The letter also said that people would be spared if they took the oath straight away.

s One of the soldiers killed a wolf rather than kill a woman and child. He showed his blood-stained sword to his officer to make him think he had obeyed the order to kill.

TASKS...

1 There are several reasons why the massacre happened.
- Some are long-term term reasons. That means they had been building up for some time.
- Some are short-term reasons. They took place a short time before the massacre.

Write down examples of both types of reason. **WS**

2 *Why was Alexander MacDonald killed?*
Use a diagram to show the long-term and short-term reasons.
Set out your diagram like this:
- A central box with the question.
- A box leading off the question box – headed *Long-term reasons*.

- Several arrows leading from the *Long-term reasons* box listing each reason.
- A second box leading off the question box – headed *Short-term reasons*.
- Several arrows leading from the *Short-term reasons* box listing each reason.

3 **a)** Use a highlighter pen to show which was the most important reason.
b) Why did you choose this reason?
c) Compare your choice with a partner. Have they made the same choice?
d) If not, explain to each other how you made your choice.

Plenary

Find two examples of how trust was broken in the story of the massacre of Glencoe. Share these with someone else in your class. See if you can end up with three examples.

Have you ever broken someone's trust? Why? What happened?

WHY DID THE UNION OF ENGLAND AND SCOTLAND TAKE PLACE?

Objectives

In this section you will find out:
- why the Union happened between England and Scotland
- what different people thought about the Union.

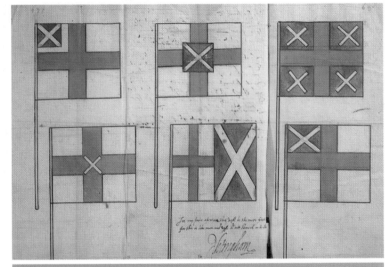

Designs for a 'British' flag in 1707.

💡 *What are the differences between the **Union** flag of 1707 and the one used today?*

💡 *Why do some football teams use the word 'united' in their name?*

Key words

Union Two or more groups joining together or uniting.

Starter
Look at the designs for a 'British' flag in 1707.

💡 *Which design do you think would have been:*
- *least favoured by the English*
- *most favoured by the English*
- *least favoured by the Scots*
- *most favoured by the Scots?*

💡 *Which design would you have chosen? Why?*

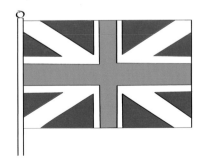

The 'Union Jack' used today.

Why did England and Scotland unite?

In the eighteenth century the Scots and the English needed important things from each other. The only way to get these was to agree to the Act of Union. Below are reasons for the Act of Union of 1707.

Protestant succession

In 1701 the English Parliament passed a law called the Act of Settlement. If William III and Mary, or Mary's younger sister, Anne, died without an heir, the English throne would go to the Protestant Sophia of Hanover or her heirs. Sophia of Hanover was the grand-daughter of James I of England (see the family tree below). This was to stop a Catholic Stuart ever becoming monarch again.

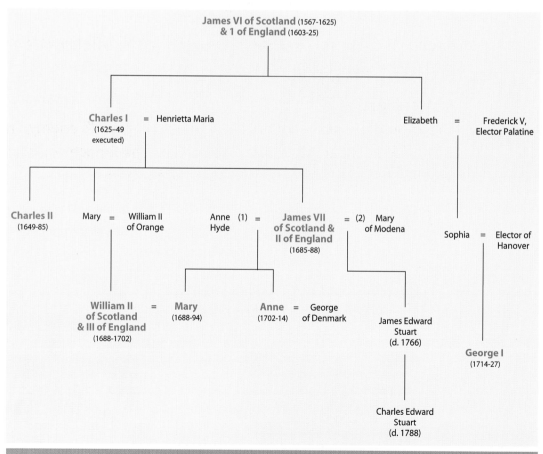

The royal family tree, 1603—1727.

The English needed the Scots to agree to the Act of Settlement. In 1704, the Scots passed an Act of Security. It said that the Scottish Parliament would jointly choose the monarch with England, and that the Scots might favour a Catholic successor to Anne.

English wealth

England was getting richer. After 1650 English farmers grew plenty of food and there were no famines. English merchants were making big profits from trade with English colonies.

Scottish poverty

Scotland had some bad harvests and people died of famine.

Scottish merchants were not allowed to trade with English colonies.

Religion

The Protestant Lowlanders in Scotland wanted the Union because they hated the Catholic Highlanders.

But not all Scots wanted the Union. The Catholic Highlanders did not want to be ruled by the Protestant English.

Fear of invasion

The English did not want Scotland to help England's enemy, France. France and Scotland had often been allies. The French could use Scotland as a base from which to attack England.

TASKS...

1 Look at the statements below. Which of them are true? Which are false? Give a reason for each answer.

- All Scottish people were for the Union.
- All English people were for the Union.
- The main reason for the Union was the problem of a successor to the English throne.
- Scottish merchants wanted the Union so they could trade with the English colonies.

2 How would these people have felt about the Act of Union:

a) an English merchant

b) a Scottish merchant wanting to trade with the Americas

c) a minister of the Scottish Presbyterian Church?

3 a) Make a copy of the graph below.

b) Plot on the graph what the different people felt about the Union.

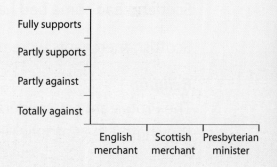

4 Make up two different headlines for the Act of Union for:

a) an English newspaper

b) a Scottish newspaper.

Remember to think who you are writing for each time.

Plenary

Which of the following is the odd one out in each group? Give a reason for each choice.

Group A:	Protestant succession	Act of Settlement	Aliens Act
Group B:	Religion	Highlanders	Presbyterian

Now, make up one group of your own. Try it out on someone else in your class.

DOOMED TO FAILURE: COULD CHARLES EDWARD STUART HAVE WON?

Objectives

In this section you will decide:
- why the **Jacobite** Rebellion of 1745 failed
- what advice you would have given to Charles Edward Stuart to help him win.

Starter

The Battle of Culloden painted by an English artist in 1746.

Key words

Jacobite A person who believed that the Stuarts (relatives of James II) were the true monarchs of England.

The road to Culloden was full of dead bodies. The English commander left the wounded with the dead on the battlefield for two days. Then he sent soldiers to kill those still alive. He ordered a barn with Highlanders in it to be set on fire.

One of Charles Edward Stuart's soldiers describing what happened after the Battle of Culloden.

💡 *What two things can you learn from Sources A and B about the Battle of Culloden?*

💡 *Neither source is totally accurate. Why do you think this is?*

Why did the Jacobite Rebellion happen in 1745?

As you read about the Jacobite Rebellion of 1745, make a note of any mistakes you think were made by Charles Edward Stuart.

Gathering support

In July 1745, Charles Edward Stuart landed on the island of Eriksay off Scotland. Charles was the grandson of King James II, who had fled to France during the 'Glorious Revolution' (see pages 85–6). He had seven men with him. Charles wanted to win the throne for his father, James Edward Stuart, and thought he would win support from the Lowlanders, who did not like paying English taxes, and the Highlanders who hated the English. He believed that the clans were looking for a reason to fight the English.

In August, Charles Edward Stuart raised his **standard** at Glenfinnan. He had 200 men. In the Highlands he won the support of some large clans. He now had 4000 men.

The English had few soldiers in Scotland.

Key words

Standard A banner or flag used in battle to indicate loyalty to a monarch.

Campbells	5000
MacKenzies	2000
Grants	850
Camerons	800
Mackintoshes	800
Frasers	900
Mackays	800
19 other clans	6800
Total	**17,950**

The fighting strength of the largest Highland clans in 1745.

SOURCE C

The Jacobite army had grown to 5500. About 4000 were real Highlanders, who were the main strength of the rebel army.

The Jacobite army as it left Edinburgh in 1745.

General Wade's Road
Prince Charles's route

The Jacobite rebellion of 1745.

The army marched to Edinburgh, the capital city. The city was captured. Charles now hoped to double the size of his army.

💡 Can you see any problems so far?

The Jacobites won a great victory near Edinburgh. Charles now had two choices:

- *either* stay in Scotland where he was popular
- *or* invade England.

His generals advised him not to invade England. They said he would not have much support there. Charles did not agree. He believed the English Catholics would support him.

💡 Have you spotted any more problems?

The invasion of England

Charles Edward Stuart marched into England. Only about 300 English Catholics joined the army. He also began to lose Scottish supporters.

Charles and his army reached Derby, only 200 km from London. His generals told him to turn back. Many Highlanders did not want to go any further. They were a long way from Scotland. They were tired, short of food and very cold.

It was said that the English army was closing in. They were thought to outnumber the Scots by six to one.

The Jacobite retreat

Charles and his Highlanders headed back to Scotland.

💡 Should Charles have turned back?

The army had a terrible march back from Derby. It was followed by the English army.

On 19 December Charles's army reached Scotland. It was getting smaller and weaker. Charles decided to split up the army to confuse the English soldiers. More and more Highlanders left the army and returned to their homes.

SOURCE D

The army when leaving Edinburgh totalled 5500 but at Carlisle totalled only 4500.

Written by Lord Elcho.

SOURCE E

Deserters leave daily from the Highland army.

From the *Evening Courant* newspaper, 8 November 1745.

SOURCE F

Every officer said the army should retreat. The prince agreed. He was sorry to be so near to London but not to be able to go on.

A meeting between Charles Edward Stuart and his generals described by one of the prince's officers.

The main part of the army defeated a small English army at Falkirk in January 1746. The Jacobites reached Stirling, but they could not capture the castle.

The Battle of Culloden

In April, the English army caught up with the Jacobites at Culloden Moor.

Charles then made more mistakes:

- His soldiers were starving on the day of the battle. Charles did not get food and drink to his men. The English soldiers had plenty to eat and drink.
- Charles went against the advice of his best commander. He told Charles to fight on soft ground nearby. This would suit the Highlanders and be too soft for the English horsemen. Charles chose to fight on the flat ground of Culloden Moor.

Charles ordered his tired men to charge. They were outnumbered and were killed by the English. At the end of the day, 1200 Jacobites and 76 English soldiers were dead.

After the battle, the English soldiers hunted down the Jacobites and killed them.

What happened after the battle?

The English decided to crush the Highlanders. Many were killed.

But Charles Edward Stuart got away. Five months later, he escaped to France.

SOURCE G

It was wrong to start the battle without knowing that the King of France would help us. It was a bad mistake to let the enemy take the best positions for their cannon and horsemen. Our army was starving.

Charles's commander Lord George Murray explained why the Highlanders lost the Battle of Culloden in a letter to Charles Edward Stuart in 1746.

TASKS...

1 What mistakes do you think were made by Charles Edward Stuart? Here are some clues to help you:
   - invasion of England
   - amount of support in England
   - amount of support in Scotland
   - the retreat from Derby
   - splitting the Jacobite army
   - Culloden.

2 Imagine that you are an adviser to Charles Edward Stuart, Sir Archie MacPherson. You know exactly what went wrong. Write a memo to Charles just before the rebellion starts. Give the prince advice on how he can win. Tell him which mistakes he must not make. Here is the start:

Memo

To: *Charles Edward Stuart*

From:

Date:

Subject:

Here is my advice before you carry out your rebellion ...

Plenary

With a partner, write down what you think are the most important facts about the Jacobite Rebellion. Share these facts with the rest of the class.

WHY DID BRITISH PEOPLE EXPLORE AND SETTLE IN DIFFERENT COUNTRIES IN THE SIXTEENTH AND SEVENTEENTH CENTURIES?

WHAT MOTIVATES EXPLORERS?

Objectives

In this section you will find out:
- why Englishmen became explorers.

Starter

Look at Sources A and B and compare the two maps. How accurate is the map of 1626?

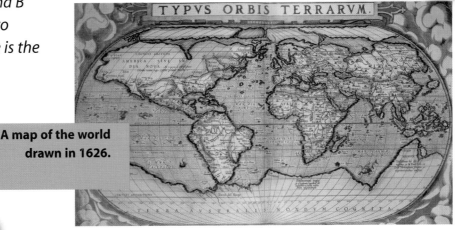

A map of the world drawn in 1626.

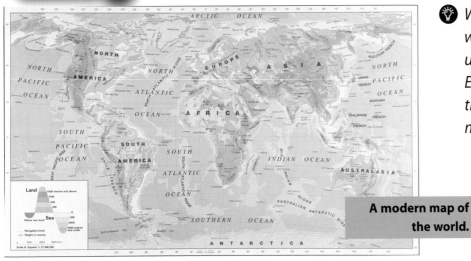

A modern map of the world.

💡 *Which parts of the world were unknown by Europeans at the time of the 1626 map.*

Why did English people start to explore in the sixteenth century?

The journeys of the great explorers

By 1521 Spanish and Portuguese explorers had found sea routes to America and the Pacific Ocean.

By 1550 the Spanish had conquered much of Central and South America. Their ships carried gold and silver back to Europe. The Portuguese also set up colonies in South America and traded with India and China.

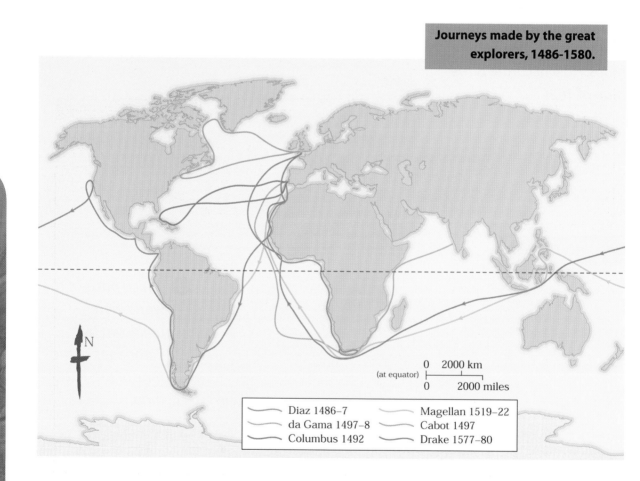

Journeys made by the great explorers, 1486-1580.

0   2000 km
(at equator)
0   2000 miles

Diaz 1486–7
da Gama 1497–8
Columbus 1492
Magellan 1519–22
Cabot 1497
Drake 1577–80

TASKS...

Read Sources C-F.

1 a) Use them to make a list of reasons why people started to explore.

b) Compare your list with someone else's in the class. See if you can both add to your lists.

2 a) Which do you think were the most important reasons?

b) Working with your partner, number the reasons in order of importance. The most important should be number 1.

c) Why do you think the reason at the top of your list was the most important?

Our loyal subject, William Penn, wishes to make the British empire larger and encourage trade in goods which may be of use to us. He also wants to take the Christian religion to the peoples of America. For this reason he has asked our permission to set up a colony in America.

Charles II's Grant of Land to William Penn, 1681.

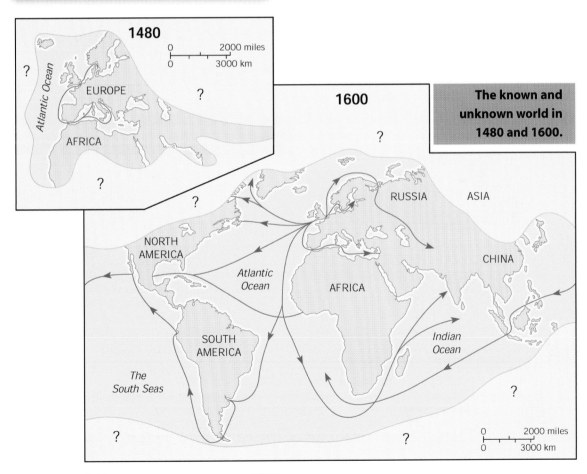

The known and unknown world in 1480 and 1600.

— English trade and exploration routes

? Unknown territory

SOURCE D

The Kings of Spain and Portugal had made their kingdoms larger. They had made themselves and their peoples richer. If we find new lands, their people will want English cloth. This will be good for the people who work in the cloth trade. Many people will be able to make things which can be traded with those who live in the new lands.

Richard Hakluyt, an English writer and clergyman, wrote about voyages of discovery during the sixteenth century.

SOURCE E

At first England had been left behind in the race for new lands. As England grew more peaceful under the Tudors, men decided to explore the world. Merchants paid for exploration which might lead to new trade. Sir Francis Drake came home in 1580 with loot taken from the Spaniards which was worth half a million pounds. He was looking for a **North-west Passage** to China and the islands where spices, silks and jewels were to be found.

From a history textbook, 1967.

SOURCE F

The first thing is to spread the news of Jesus Christ to those who know nothing of Him. The second is to teach the natives about farming. Then we need to see what lands can be found by sailing to the north-east. It would be good to have our own trade routes to India and China. This will bring great riches.

Richard Hakluyt, writing in the sixteenth century.

Key words

North-west Passage A sea passage along the north coast of North America linking the Atlantic and Pacific Oceans.

Plenary

Think up two meanings of the word 'exploration'. Ask someone else in the class to choose the better meaning.

WHAT MAKES THE PERFECT EXPLORER?

Objectives

In this section you will find out:
- what explorers were like
- why they wanted to explore.

Starter

If you were about to go on a journey to explore the world, which ten things would you take with you?

Which of these things would not have been around in the sixteenth and seventeenth centuries?

What problems would this have caused for the explorers? How did they manage without them?

Read the following account of the adventures of Sir Francis Drake.

The adventures of Sir Francis Drake

In December 1577 five ships left Plymouth. In front was the Pelican, later called the Golden Hind. The 164 men who sailed with Drake did not know where they were going. Drake told them they were going to the Mediterranean Sea. He knew that many of them would have been afraid to sail had they known the truth.

As they crossed the equator, the weather was very hot and some sailors talked about **mutiny**.

When the ships reached the Magellan Straits in South America, two of them broke up. The others sailed for 500 kilometres through the most dangerous seas in the world. The weather remained fine and the ships reached the Pacific Ocean.

Then the weather changed. There was a storm and another ship sank. A fourth, the Elizabeth, lost touch with the Golden Hind and sailed back to England. The Golden Hind sailed north up the coast of South America. Drake heard that a Spanish treasure ship was nearby. He caught up with it, boarded the ship and took treasure chests full of gold, silver and jewels.

Key words

Mutiny Refusal to obey the orders of an officer.

 What famous mutinies can you think of?

The Golden Hind then sailed for home. Drake sailed north and landed on the coast of North America. Here they met a tribe of friendly Indians who thought Drake was a god.

Drake set sail again, but the Golden Hind ran aground. Guns and stores were thrown overboard to lighten the ship.

Drake returned home in September 1580. Queen Elizabeth came on board the Golden Hind and knighted him Sir Francis Drake.

TASKS...

1 Imagine you are a sailor on the *Golden Hind*.

   a) Write down the two events you remember most.

   b) Ask someone else in the class which two they chose. Were they the same or different choices?

2 Work in groups. You work for an employment agency in England in 1595. Queen Elizabeth has asked you to find an explorer to look for the North-west Passage.

   Read the following information about famous explorers. Make a note of anything that you think is important to be an explorer.

Profiles of some famous explorers

John Cabot

Cabot was an Italian. He came to England in 1494. Like Columbus, he planned to sail west across the Atlantic to look for the Spice Islands of Asia.

Key words

New World The name for the parts of South and Central America first explored by Spanish and Portuguese sailors.

Cabot asked Henry VII of England to pay for the trip. Henry knew of the riches of the **New World**. He agreed to support Cabot so that he could make money from any discoveries.

In May 1497 Cabot set sail from Bristol. He was brave to sail to a part of the world that no one in Europe knew. A month later, he landed in Newfoundland, off the east coast of Canada. He claimed this new land for England. He also found rich fishing grounds.

Sir Walter Raleigh

Sir Walter Raleigh was one of Queen Elizabeth I's favourite **courtiers**. He was a soldier and a sailor.

Sir Walter Raleigh in 1585.

Raleigh knew that the Spaniards had found gold and silver in America. He wanted to do the same. Between 1584 and 1587 Raleigh made four voyages to North America. He explored the coast between present-day Florida and North Carolina. He called this land Virginia, after Queen Elizabeth (the 'Virgin Queen'), and tried to set up colonies there.

Raleigh brought potatoes and tobacco back to England. They soon became very popular.

In 1595 Raleigh set out for South America. He was looking for El Dorado, the city of gold. He did not find it. After Queen Elizabeth died, James I put Raleigh in prison. In 1617, the king gave Raleigh a last chance to find El Dorado. He failed and was executed.

Key words

Courtier A person who attends the king or queen in a royal court.

Sir Francis Drake

Drake was one of 12 children. His father was a poor farm worker. Drake became an apprentice on ships in the English Channel. Later he began attacking Spanish ships and became known as a clever and brave **privateer**. Drake was really a pirate, but he attacked England's enemy, Spain, so Queen Elizabeth liked him. He returned to England with lots of gold, stolen from the Spanish.

A portrait of Sir Francis Drake.

On his return home from his voyage of 1577–80, Drake was welcomed as a hero. He was only the second person to have gone around the world.

Drake bought a big house with money from his trips. He became Mayor of Portsmouth and then an MP. Drake was very brave. He would lead attacks on Spanish ships and took great risks to win riches and fame.

In 1587 he led an expedition to attack the Spanish Armada while it was in port. Drake set fire to the fleet and destroyed some of its ships. In the following year, Drake took part in the fight against the Spanish Armada.

In 1595 Drake tried to take the island of Gran Canaria from the Spanish. He failed, became ill and died.

Key word

Privateer A commander of his own ship who is paid by the government to attack the ships of another country.

Henry Hudson

Hudson was an Englishman and an expert navigator (sea explorer). He wanted to explore North America and find the North-west Passage.

In 1609, Hudson discovered a big river on the east coast of America. It was named the Hudson River after him. In 1610, he bravely sailed his ship round northern Canada before heading south towards what he hoped would be the Pacific Ocean. It turned out to be a large bay, which was named after him – the Hudson Bay.

Hudson was not put off by this problem and wanted to sail on, but his crew refused. In June 1611 they mutinied and put Hudson and his loyal crew in an open boat with no oars. They were left to die.

Hudson had explored many areas of Canada which later became English colonies.

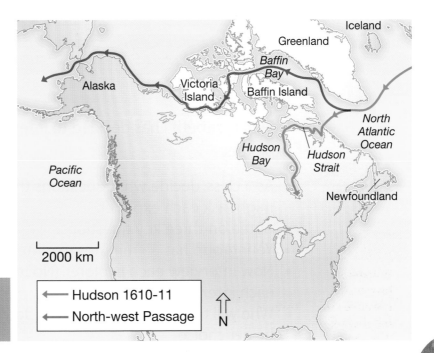

The North-west Passage and Henry Hudson's journey of 1610–11.

TASKS...

Work in groups.

1 Each group should now choose an explorer. Write a letter to Queen Elizabeth I, applying for the job of explorer to the North-west Passage. The letter will go with your **CV**.

- You need to show that your explorer is the best person for the job. Remember to stress his best qualities.
- Write about the things the explorer has done and his successes.

Here is a writing frame to help you with your letter.
You could do this on a computer.

> Name of explorer
> Make up an address
> Date – some time in 1595
>
> Dear Queen Elizabeth
>
> I am writing for the job of explorer. I think you should choose me because I have the qualities needed to explore. These are …
>
> I am also a good choice because of my past experience and successes. These include …
>
> Yours sincerely
>
>
> Sign your name

Plenary

Queen Elizabeth I has decided to interview each of the explorers.

- As a class, decide what questions the queen (your teacher) might ask each explorer.
- Agree on three key questions.
- Your group has 15 minutes to write answers to each question.
- Now interview each explorer. (No more than two minutes for each interview.)
- Who will the queen choose? Why do you think this person will be her choice?

WHY DID BRITISH PEOPLE EMIGRATE TO THE COLONIES?

Objectives

In this chapter you will look at:
- why people decided to live in Britain's new colonies.

Key words

Emigrate To leave your own country to go and live in another.
Colonies Countries ruled by another country.
Civilised A place which is advanced in its way of living.

Starter

*Read Source A. William Bradford gives two reasons why people should not **emigrate** to the **colonies**. Who do you think are the 'wild men' he talks about?*

They had no friends to welcome them, no houses. It was winter. All they could see was a wild country, full of wild beasts and wild men. If they looked behind them there was the ocean between them and all the **civilised** parts of the world.

The settler William Bradford wrote about what it was like to arrive in the American colonies in 1620.

💡 *Give two reasons from Source A why people should not emigrate to the colonies.*

💡 *Would you want to emigrate to somewhere like this? Why?*

Why people emigrated: the evidence

In the seventeenth century many people from Britain went to North America to live on land which seemed to belong to no one. The map on page 208 shows where British people settled in North America during the seventeenth century.

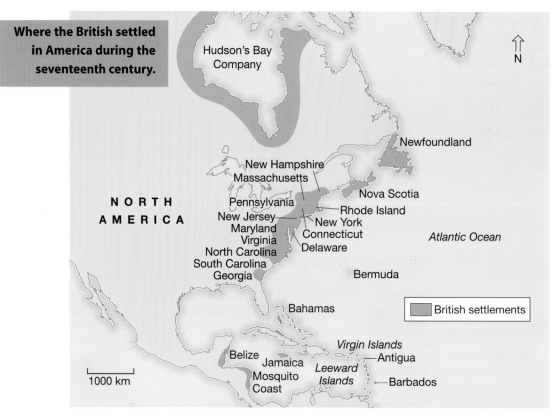

Where the British settled in America during the seventeenth century.

Hudson's Bay Company

Newfoundland

New Hampshire
Massachusetts

Nova Scotia

NORTH AMERICA

Pennsylvania
New Jersey
Maryland
Virginia
North Carolina
South Carolina
Georgia

Rhode Island
New York
Connecticut
Delaware

Atlantic Ocean

Bermuda

Bahamas

British settlements

Belize
Jamaica
Mosquito Coast

Virgin Islands
Antigua

Leeward Islands

Barbados

N

1000 km

TASKS...

1 Why did people go to live in the colonies? The table below gives some reasons. Copy and complete the table.

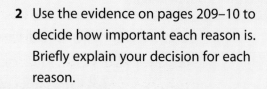

2 Use the evidence on pages 209–10 to decide how important each reason is. Briefly explain your decision for each reason.

Reason for emigrating	Strongly agree	Agree	Disagree	Strongly disagree
To find gold				
To make money by selling things to settlers				
To get away from hard work				
To get away from renting farmland				
To find a more healthy place to live				
To find more freedom				
Lack of religious tolerance in England				
To do something different and exciting				
To teach the local people their ways				
To bring Christianity to the local peoples				
Any other reason				

TASKS...

3 Now separate the reasons into push and pull factors:
- Push factors are bad things about England which make them want to leave.
- Pull factors are good things about the New World which make them want to go there.

Who settled in North America?

Most of the settlers were working people. They hoped to make a better living in the New World. There was a chance, too, that there were fortunes to be made, but many of them had other reasons for giving up their homes.

What were their reasons for emigrating?

Many people wanted the freedom to practise their religion. Puritans settled in New England. Maryland was founded by Catholics.

Others wanted to 'civilise' the local peoples. They wanted to teach them European ways of living and about Christianity.

Many country people wanted good, cheap farming land. They could not afford to buy land in England. In America there was land for everyone. In Virginia the settlers learned to grow tobacco. Smoking was a new habit in Europe and tobacco was in demand. Rich people came over from England and bought up lots of land for growing tobacco.

SOURCE B

It will be serving the Church ... to take Christianity into these parts of the world.

A Puritan settler writing in 1712.

Convict A person who has been found guilty of a crime and is being punished for that crime.

Vagrant A person who has no home or job and wanders from place to place looking for food and shelter.

Some settlers wanted to take part in government instead of having to do as kings told them. However, many settlers were disappointed as rulers in the New World were sometimes as strict as rulers in Europe.

Convicts and **vagrants** were often sent to the colonies as slaves and servants.

TASKS...

1 Three people are getting ready to sail to North America. They meet for the first time and explain to each other their reasons for moving to the New World. The group includes:

- a farmer
- a Puritan
- a merchant.

Put together a conversation between these people. Include as many reasons as you can.

a) *Either* write out the conversation

b) *or* draw a picture of each person and use speech bubbles.

For example:

> A Puritan called ... said, 'I am moving to the New World because...'
>
> The farmer who was called ... said, 'I am going for different reasons. These are ...'

Plenary

What is the most interesting thing you have learned in this section?

Share this with someone else in your class. Did they have the same answer as you?

WHO BENEFITED FROM THE COLONIES AND THE BRITISH EMPIRE?

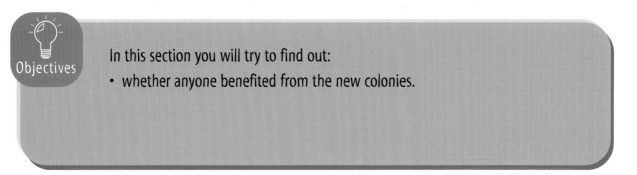

Objectives

In this section you will try to find out:
• whether anyone benefited from the new colonies.

Starter

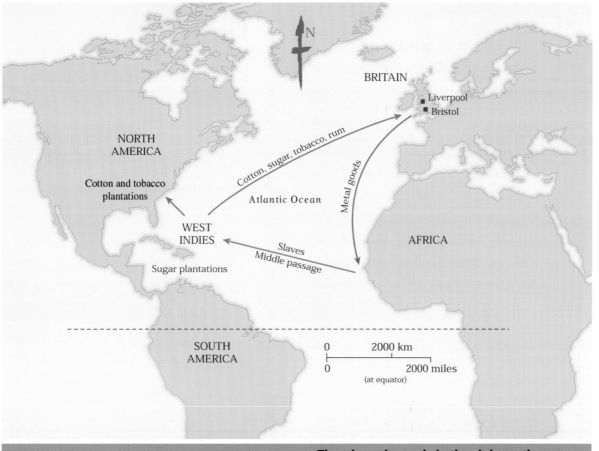

The triangular trade in the eighteenth century.

Draw your own diagram to show how the triangular trade worked between England, West Africa and the West Indies.

💡 *Why do you think the slave and sugar merchants organised the trade in this way?*

What were the benefits and disadvantages of exploration and settlement?

TASKS...

1 Look at Sources A-I. Make a copy of the table below.

   a) Which sources show that people benefited from the colonies? Write these in the table. Briefly explain your choice.

   b) Which sources show that people suffered? Write these in the table and explain your choice.

   One example has been done for you.

Sources showing benefits	Sources showing disadvantages
Source F – because British merchants got more trade	

SOURCE A

A crew of pirates are in a storm. Soon a boy spots land and they go on shore to rob. They find a kind people who welcome them. They give the country a new name, they take it for their king and they kill many of its people. This is a modern colony.

An extract from Jonathan Swift's *Gulliver's Travels*, written in 1726.

SOURCE B

The dockside at Bristol. In the seventeenth and eighteenth centuries Bristol became the second largest English city after London. Its wealth came from trade with the colonies.

British traders were part of the slave trade. British ships took Africans as slaves to America. There they worked for their owners growing cotton and sugar, which were then shipped back to Britain. It made money for the British, but at great human cost.

From a modern textbook.

The Africans were so sad to leave their country that they often leapt out of the ships into the sea, and stayed under water until they drowned. We had about 12 Africans who drowned themselves, for they believe that when they die they return home to their country and friends. Some captains cut off the arms and legs of some slaves to scare the rest.

The captain of a British slave-ship in 1693.

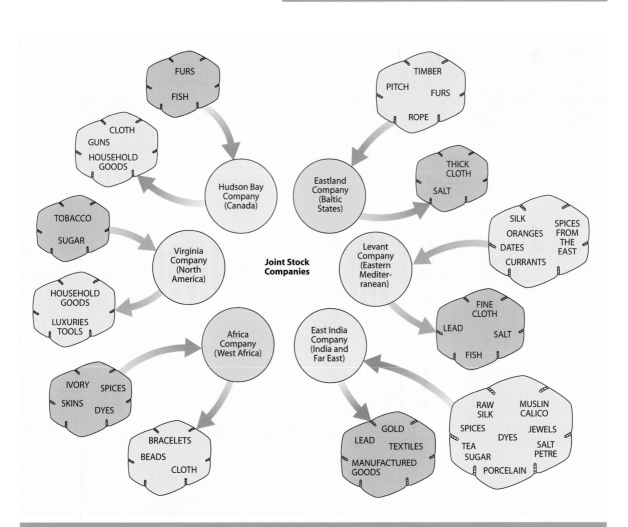

British companies which traded with the British Empire.

A drawing of a slave being branded.

SOURCE F

The colonies brought new goods – sugar from the West Indies, silks and cottons from the East, and spices from all over the world. New crops like potatoes and tobacco were introduced to Britain. Tea and coffee had been unknown in Britain before 1500.

The new trade made Britain very powerful.

From a modern textbook.

SOURCE G

A painting of a coffee house in the seventeenth century.

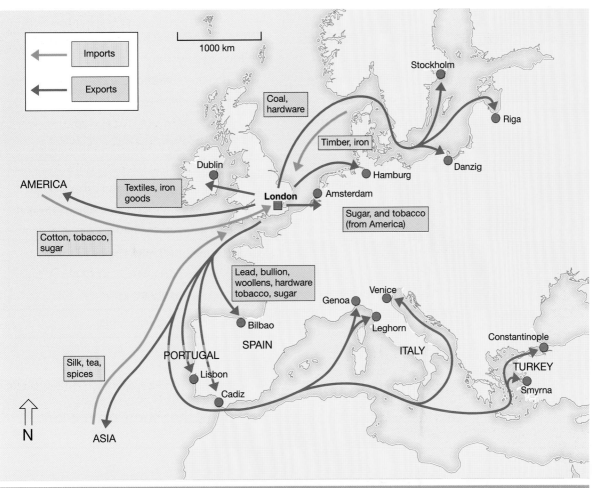

British imports and exports in the seventeenth century.

Map labels:
- Imports
- Exports
- 1000 km
- Coal, hardware
- Stockholm
- Riga
- Timber, iron
- Danzig
- Hamburg
- Dublin
- AMERICA
- Textiles, iron goods
- London
- Amsterdam
- Sugar, and tobacco (from America)
- Cotton, tobacco, sugar
- Lead, bullion, woollens, hardware tobacco, sugar
- Venice
- Genoa
- Leghorn
- Constantinople
- Bilbao
- SPAIN
- ITALY
- TURKEY
- Smyrna
- Silk, tea, spices
- PORTUGAL
- Lisbon
- Cadiz
- N
- ASIA

SOURCE H

Owned by James Stone	Value
Thomas Groves, 4 years to serve	1300 lbs of tobacco
Emaniel, a black slave	2000 lbs tobacco
Mingo, a black slave	2000 lbs of tobacco

From a list of the property of a colonist in 1648.

SOURCE I

By 1750 in Britain you could buy apricots, avocados, bananas, beetroot, kidney beans, melons, peaches, peanuts, pineapples, potatoes, tomatoes, turkeys and gin. The main import goods were chocolate, coffee, cotton, sugar, tea and tobacco. It became fashionable to drink coffee or hot chocolate in one of the new coffee-houses while smoking a pipe. Some rich people also had a black slave.

From a modern textbook.

TASKS...

1 Write down your answers to the following questions:

   a) Who do you think benefited from the empire? What evidence is there?

   b) Who do you think lost out due to the empire? What evidence is there?

2 Imagine that there was television in the early eighteenth century. You are putting together a programme on the benefits of the colonies and the British Empire. You interview the following people:

   - a British merchant
   - a British settler in North America
   - a slave in the West Indies.

Write out how each would answer the following question:

How do you think that the British Empire has affected your life?

Here is how to start your interviews.

Today I am interviewing some people to try to find out who has benefited from the British Empire. I asked three people – a British merchant, a British settler and a slave – the same question:

How do you think the British Empire has affected your life?

Here is what each of them said.

The British merchant called ... said ...

Plenary

Design a simple web page that sums up the key points of today's lesson.

THEME: EXTERNAL RELATIONS

CONCLUSION

You have seen in this theme that between 1500 and 1750 England was becoming a more powerful country. There were arguments with neighbouring countries, Scotland and Ireland. Wars were fought with France and Spain. Some of the unknown parts of the world were explored and English people started to colonise the 'New World' of America.

You can now complete your timeline for 1500-1750 by plotting the important events in England's relations with the rest of the world. You could add them under three headings: 'Ireland and Scotland', 'Europe' and 'Exploration and Colonisation'. When you have finished, use highlighter pens to show whether each of the changes or developments was a success for England, a failure, or neither. Use green for success, red for failure and yellow for neither.

An example has been done for you below.

Date	1620	1630	1640	1650	1660	1670	1680	1690
Ruler				Charles I/Parliament				
Main Religion				Protestant				
Political Events				Civil War				
Changes in people's lives				Witch trials,1640s				
Threats and Opportunities	**Threats:** Poor diet; childbirth			**Threats:** Puritan rule			**Opportunities:** New industries; growing towns	
Ireland and Scotland							Battle of the Boyne	
Europe		War against France						
Exploration and Colonisation	Pilgrim Fathers							

When you have finished your timeline you will be able to see for yourself why these really were 'Revolutionary Times'!

Index